MOCTEZUMA'S MEXICO

MOCTEZUMA'S MEXICO

Visions of the Aztec World

by

DAVÍD CARRASCO *and* EDUARDO MATOS MOCTEZUMA

SCOTT SESSIONS
Assistant Editor

Foreword by
JAMES N. CORBRIDGE, Jr.

With Essays by
ANTHONY F. AVENI *and* ELIZABETH HILL BOONE

Photographs by
SALVADOR GUIL'LIEM ARROYO

UNIVERSITY PRESS OF COLORADO

Copyright © 1992 by the University Press of Colorado
P.O. Box 849
Niwot, Colorado 80544

10 9 8 7 6 5 4 3 2 1

The University Press of Colorado is a cooperative publishing
enterprise supported, in part, by Adams State College, Colorado
State University, Fort Lewis College, Mesa State College, Metropolitan State College of Denver, University of Colorado, University of Northern Colorado, University of Southern Colorado, and
Western State College.

Library of Congress Cataloging-in-Publication Data

Carrasco, Davíd
    Moctezuma's Mexico: visions of the Aztec world / by Davíd
Carrasco and Eduardo Matos Moctezuma; Scott Sessions, assis-
tant editor; foreword by James N. Corbridge, Jr.; with essays by
Anthony F. Aveni and Elizabeth Hill Boone; photographs by
Salvador Guil'liem Arroyo.
        p.   cm.
    Includes bibliographical references and index.
    ISBN 0-87081-263-7
    1. Aztecs — History.   2. Aztecs — Social life and customs.
3. Aztecs — Antiquities.   4. Mexico — Antiquities.   I. Matos
Moctezuma, Eduardo.   II. Sessions, Scott.   III. Title.
F1219.73.C36 1992
972'.018 —dc20   92-11993
                                                      CIP

The paper used in this publication meets the minimum require-
ments of the American National Standard for Information Sci-
ences—Permanence of Paper for Printed Library Materials. ANSI
Z39.48–1984

Illustrations of the *Codex Mendoza* are reprinted from the facsimile
edition edited by James Cooper Clark (London: Waterlow and
Sons, Ltd., 1938) of the original manuscript in the Bodleian
Library, Oxford, England.

Cover: Tlaloc ceramic vessel, Museo del Templo Mayor (photograph by Salvador Guil'liem Arroyo).

Endpapers: "The Great City of Tenochtitlan," Diego Rivera Mural,
Palacio Nacional, México D.F. (photograph by Scott Sessions).

Design: Carol Humphrey

Printed in Italy.

CONTENTS

ILLUSTRATIONS

FOREWORD

Almost five hundred years have passed since Hernan Cortés and his Spanish conquistadores landed at Mexico and began the conquest of an Aztec empire that astonished them with its architectural wonders. Today the cultural achievements of the Aztecs remain obscured by a historical fascination with the human sacrifices and warlike behavior that characterized the Aztec society observed by Cortés and recorded by his army ser geant and chronicler, Bernal Díaz del Castillo. Human offerings to the gods, including the tearing of beating hearts from the victims' breasts, were common to the rituals of religious life of the empire. Perhaps, not surprisingly, these rituals shocked the Spanish and have, until recently, dominated the attention of subsequent generations of Mesoamerican scholars. Underappreciated are the pictorial writings, poetry, and myths, along with the ceramics, sculpture, and architecture that seem all the more impressive in the apparent absence of metal tools.

Beginning with their migration from Aztlan, the mythical "place of reeds and herons" and site of origin, the Aztecs went on to found the great capital city of Tenochtitlan, and then to expand their imperial hegemony over the greater part of Mesoamerica.

The island city of Tenochtitlan, which lay at the spiritual center of an empire the Aztecs considered as being without geographical limit, was the architectural crown of a great urban society. Along with its gemstone, the Templo Mayor, or the Great Temple, the city was a center of activities that included crafts, trade, and agriculture. Roads

radiated into the empire, and an aqueduct system imported potable water to the citizens of a thriving commercial, political, and religious community of around 150,000 inhabitants.

Recent investigations of the Great Temple, and of Tenochtitlan's neighboring commercial city and temple of Tlatelolco, have uncovered a wealth of archaeological material. Many of these artifacts were brought together in a major exhibit at the Denver Museum of Natural History. Their exhibit was made possible by the collaborative efforts of the Denver Museum of Natural History, the Museum of the Great Temple in Mexico City, and the University of Colorado, and represented a milestone in a continuing interdisciplinary endeavor of scientific, archaeological, and cultural inquiry into Mesoamerican civilization — designed to shed new light on the religious, artistic, political, and commercial achievements of the Aztecs. This book has been written by four distinguished Mesoamerican scholars, each of whom has made major contributions to that inquiry: Anthony Aveni of Colgate University, Elizabeth Hill Boone of Dumbarton Oaks, Davíd Carrasco of the University of Colorado at Boulder, and Eduardo Matos Moctezuma, distinguished archaeologist and director of the Museum of the Great Temple.

The collaboration between the University of Colorado and the Proyecto Templo Mayor in Mexico has further stimulated Aztec studies over the past fifteen years. The relationship between the two institutions began with the excavation of the Great Temple, coordinated by Dr. Matos following the discovery by electrical workers of the Coyolxauhqui

Stone under the streets of Mexico City in 1978. In addition to the sponsorship of several important scholarly conferences, university support was provided for archaeological excavations at the temple of the marketplace center at Tlatelolco (Proyecto Tlatelolco). This in turn led to exhibits at both El Museo del Templo Mayor and at the Denver Museum of Natural History ("Lord of the Wind: Aztec Offerings at Tlatelolco"), which laid the foundation for the powerful "Aztec: The World of Moctezuma" exhibit.

As this book indicates, large gaps characterize our knowledge of the Aztec world. The murals of Tlatelolco need further study, as does the meaning of the Aztec rites and the identification of their astronomical constellations. What was the role of the tradesmen (*pochteca*) in the expansion of the empire? What is the meaning of the mythical return of Quetzalcoatl? These and many other scholarly puzzles remain unsolved. The interdisciplinary approach represented in the exhibit, "Aztec: The World of Moctezuma," and in this book may hold the key to unlocking the secrets of the Aztecs.

JAMES N. CORBRIDGE, JR.
Chancellor
University of Colorado at Boulder

PREFACE

A COMMUNITY OF INTERPRETERS

One of the significant academic achievements in Aztec studies of the last decade has unfolded through a collaboration between the University of Colorado and Proyecto Templo Mayor of the Instituto Nacional de Antropología in Mexico City. This collaboration began within months after the stunning discovery of the famous Coyolxauhqui Stone beneath the street behind the National Cathedral in 1978. During my visit to the site in May of that year Eduardo Matos Moctezuma and I began to develop plans for interdisciplinary studies of the fabulous treasures being uncovered daily at the Templo Mayor. Then, in October of 1979 the University of Colorado, through the leadership of the Department of Religion, hosted the first scholarly conference on the new discoveries titled "Center and Periphery: The Great Temple and the Aztec Empire." This conference, attended by many of the leading scholars in the field of Aztec and urban studies (including Pedro Armillas, Alfredo Lopez Austin, H. B. Nicholson, and Paul Wheatley),[1] focused on the temple and economic tribute, human sacrifice and ideology, spatial symbolism in Teotihuacan and Tenochtitlan, magical flight, and Mesoamerican cosmology. We were inspired by the guidance and generosity of Eduardo Matos who eventually directed the excavation of over seven thousand ritual objects at the Templo Mayor.

As a result of the remarkable intellectual chemistry at this conference, Eduardo Matos and I took two steps toward forming a community of interpreters and establishing a long-term research center at the University of Colorado's Mesoamerican Archive and Research Center. First, we decided, with the help of Lawrence G. Desmond, a Mesoamerican anthropologist and photographer, to establish a photographic collection of the Templo Mayor discoveries. The University of Colorado, through the president's office, provided funds to photograph and collect over 7,000 photographs of Proyecto Templo Mayor for research purposes. This research center also contains over one thousand articles representing the state of the art in research on sacred space, human sacrifice, archaeoastronomy, Aztec religion, Maya ceremonial centers, colonialism, and theoretical approaches to Mesoamerican religions. Also, we have benefited from the distinctive research projects by three of our research associates, Robert Bye, Edelmira Linares, and Robert Carlsen. Bye and Linares carry out research in the Mexican market plants of the sixteenth century and their presence in contemporary market systems in Mexico. Carlsen's work on the ritual life of the Ateteco Maya of Santiago Atitlan has extended the archive focus into contemporary manifestations of Mesoamerican cosmovision.

Second, we began to plan a series of research conferences organized by an interdisciplinary agenda inspired by both the archaeology of the Templo Mayor and the interpretive frameworks of the history of religions. Fortunately, the Mesoamerican Archive, established in 1984, received a generous grant from Raphael and Fletcher Lee Moses to support ten years of research seminars on such topics as center and periphery dynamics in Aztec religion, religious performance and ceremonial landscapes in Mesoamerica, and archaeoastronomy and religion in the Aztec world. The last theme was nurtured by the presence of Anthony Aveni, the productive astronomer and anthropologist from Colgate University who helped me in organizing some of the activities at the University of Colorado. Johanna Broda's synthetic studies of Aztec ceremonial life enlarged our vision of the Aztec world. The distinguished historian of religions, Charles Long, enriched the methodological and interpretive design of the research meetings.

This work of photographic and interpretive research was greatly enhanced when the University of Colorado, through the Mesoamerican Archive, funded three years of excavations at the ceremonial center of Tlatelolco that served as the imperial marketplace of the Aztec empire from 1473 to 1521. This work was carried out by Eduardo Matos's remarkable archaeological team, which made a number of significant discoveries allowing us to begin comparative reflections on the symbolism and burial patterns at the two Templo Mayors, that is, at Tenochtitlan and Tlatelolco.

This project resulted in a wonderful exhibition in Mexico City's Museo del Templo Mayor titled "Excavaciones Recientes en Tlatelolco" and visited by over 1 million people in 1988. Professor Matos and I, along with the support of Lois Middleton, Archive Administrator, agreed to expand our project by working with the Denver Museum of Natural History, where the archaeologist Jane Stevenson Day had been developing projects in Mesoamerican cultures. This new collaboration resulted in "Lord of the Wind: Aztec Offerings at Tlatelolco, Mexico" in 1989 at the Denver Museum.

The success of that exhibition laid the groundwork for the planning of "Aztec: The World of Moctezuma," the largest and most impressive exhibition of purely Aztec materials in the United States. This exhibition resulted from a special decade of collaboration between the University of Colorado and the Instituto Nacional de Antropología e Historia in Mexico City, and now the Denver Museum of Natural History.

The scholarly collaboration centered in the Mesoamerican Archive in Boulder, but also extending through the "Archive on Wheels" to such places as Colgate University, University of California at Los Angeles, Dumbarton Oaks, Cocotitlan, and the cliffs of Chalcatzingo, Mexico, resulted in a number of publications, most notably *The Imagination of Matter: Religion and Ecology in Mesoamerican Traditions* and most recently, *To Change Place: Aztec Ceremonial Landscapes,* both edited by Davíd Carrasco. The latter book, published by the University Press of Colorado, contains some of the newest Aztec discoveries in Mexico as well as an original series of articles on new understandings of Aztec ceremonial life.

As these results show, there is much waiting for the visitor on holiday and the scholar in the ruins of the great ceremonial spaces of Mexico City. Carlos Fuentes said it best when he wrote that Mexico City was a "city of the true image of gigantic heaven." This gigantic city and its heaven were the confines of Moctezuma's world; it is a world we will return to again and again in person and through the pages of this book.

NOTE

1. Participants in the 1979 conference at the University of Colorado included José Arguellas, Pedro Armillas, Johanna Broda, Davíd Carrasco, Edward Calnek, José Cuellar, Wilfred Gingerrich, Richard Hecht, Doris Heyden, John Hoag, Alfredo López Austin, Eduardo Matos Moctezuma, Henry B. Nicholson, Esther Pasztory, Payson Sheets, Paul Shankman, William B. Taylor, and Paul Wheatley. Also participating from the Department of Religious Studies were Frederick Denny, Ira Chernus, Robert Lester, and Rodney Taylor.

MOCTEZUMA'S MEXICO

INTRODUCTION

It is a difficult but gratifying task to introduce one of ancient Mexico's great civilizations: the Aztecs. It is a difficult task because this is the group about which the most has been written from the sixteenth century to the present day. A large number of written documents have come to us from different chroniclers. The soldier-chronicler gave us his vision of the war of conquest, while the friar examined in depth the customs, ceremonies, and general characteristics of the Aztec people with the goal of knowing their world and carrying out his evangelizing work. Of great importance are the chronicles of the descendants of Indian women and Spaniards, who knew their maternal language — Nahuatl — and who narrate for us important passages from the history of this society. To this must be added a series of legends and myths transcribed into Nahuatl and written in that language in the Spanish alphabet. So an accumulation of diverse data allows us to approach this society.

But these are not the only existing sources. We also have the invaluable archaeological data that permit us to witness the world of Moctezuma. Thus, for two hundred years — from the thirteenth of August 1790, when the monumental statue of Coatlicue, mother of the gods, was discovered, until today, when the Great Temple Project continues to provide new data — the archaeology of the Mexica has been an inexhaustible source of information through which the ceramics, stonework, sculpture, architecture, painting, and many other elements speak to us of an agrarian and warrior society. This society was equally able to conquer distant regions and write poetry expressing the profound feelings of a people who based their very existence on agricultural production and on the worship of the gods who permitted the growth of plants; a people for whom war was the essential means of imposing tribute on other groups and was a reflection of the destiny of their warrior god, Huitzilopochtli.

In what follows we give a historical profile of the Aztec people and illustrate a number of their ritual, mythic, and symbolic traditions. To make a compendium of the history and religion of this society within the pages of a single book is not possible; much data must necessarily remain unexplored. To assist in this challenge, we are pleased to present essays by two of our colleagues, Anthony Aveni and Elizabeth Boone, whose research and writing on Aztec astronomy and migrations, skyscapes, and landscapes enlarge our understanding of Moctezuma's glorious imperium. We also summarize here the necessity and character of an important interdisciplinary project organized jointly by the Mesoamerican Archive at the University of Colorado and the Proyecto Templo Mayor, which is part of the Instituto Nacional de Antropología e Historia in Mexico City. Participants in this project have developed new approaches to and new understandings of the world of Moctezuma. We hope that the little that is said here will stir the reader to dig more deeply into the primary sources and the more extensive treatises that have been written about the Aztecs. If we achieve that interest, then we will be satisfied and our desire will be fulfilled: to be, simply, a small key that serves to open a view of the history, archaeology, and cosmovision of one Mesoamerican culture whose fate was that of confronting the European conquest: the Aztecs of central Mexico.

EDUARDO MATOS MOCTEZUMA
DAVÍD CARRASCO

AZTEC HISTORY AND COSMOVISION

EDUARDO MATOS MOCTEZUMA

THE ORIGIN OF THE AZTECS

The place of origin of the Aztecs has not been located with precision. History and myth are mixed in such a way that it is not easy to say whether they came from some northern place outside the Valley of Mexico or, as other investigators believe, that they actually dwelled there already. The majority of the sixteenth-century chronicles that speak of this group agree that they came from the north, from a place called Aztlan, which — though difficult to translate from Nahuatl — in some interpretations means "place of the storks" or "of whiteness." It seems that around A.D. 1000 the Aztecs inhabited that region, which may well have been dominated and controlled by the Toltecs, a group who by that time had their capital city in Tula and exercised extensive control over various regions. The Aztecs possibly paid tribute to the Toltecs in the forms of goods, services, and obedience. We know through historical sources that the Toltec empire had begun to suffer disasters and was weakening. The Aztecs and other subject groups may have taken advantage of this fact to begin their liberation from Tula, which was finally destroyed around A.D. 1165.

Chroniclers such as Diego Durán, Fernando Alvarado Tezozomóc, and Bernal Díaz del Castillo provide valuable information about Aztec life during the period when the Aztecs inhabited Aztlan, or about the moment in which they left their community to begin their journey. If these descriptions are correct, we must believe that they were a Mesoamericanized group, that is, an agricultural society already incorporating the *chinampa,* the system of intensive cultivation of lake environments; that they were socially stratified into clans with astronomical/calendrical knowledge, elaborate rituals, and a complex cosmovision, but were subservient to the Toltec state. The picture is not that of a barbarous people, which is often presented to us.

Other researchers have pointed out the interesting similarity between Aztlan and Mexico-Tenochtitlan, the city they founded much later in the Valley of Mexico, a similarity that suggests that the former may well have been a kind of prototype for the latter. Both communities are in the middle of a lake; there is a neighboring settlement — Cohualtepec at Aztlan and Tlatelolco at Tenochtitlan; they are divided into districts; and the residents are familiar with the chinampa, the system of productive agriculture; in sum, there are similarities so surprising that some authors postulate an archetype for both cities. Be that as it may, the important fact is that with both myth and history we can only sketch the outlines of the earliest Aztec settlements.

Nevertheless, the mythical traditions tell us that, being in Aztlan, the god Huitzilopochtli

3

Monumental Toltec warriors from the ceremonial site at Tula. Basalt sculptures.

(Hummingbird on the Left), the principal god of the Aztecs, appeared to the priests in visions and told them that they should undertake a pilgrimage and head toward the south, where they would find a new land to inhabit. An ancient song tells the story:

As they came,
as they went along their road,
they were no longer received anywhere,
they were rejected everywhere,
no one knew their face.
Everywhere they were asked:
"Who are you?

4

Temple of Tlahuizcalpantecuhtli at Tula, dedicated to the planet Venus, an apparition of Quetzalcoatl, the Feathered Serpent.

From where do you come?"
Thus nowhere could they settle,
they were always thrown out,
everywhere were they persecuted.
They passed through Coatepec,
they passed through Tollan,
they passed through Ichpuchco,
they passed through Ecatepec,
thence to Chiquiuhtepetitlan.
Next, to Chapultepec
where many peoples came to settle.

And there was a kingdom in Azcapotzalco,
and in Coatlinchan,
but Mexico did not yet exist,
there still were fields of bulrushes and reeds
where now is Mexico.[1]

Who was this god Huitzilopochtli? Apparently, as happens in many societies, an outstanding governor or leader was deified upon his death. Such, it appears, was the case with this god. Cristóbal del Castillo, chronicler of the sixteenth

Chicomoztoc, the "Seven Caves," and the beginning of the Mexica migration, from the *Codex Durán,* Museo Nacional de Antropología, México, D.F.

century, tells us the god was originally a personage called Huitzil, priest of the god Tetzauhteotl (the prodigy god), who would later lead the departure from Aztlan. After a time the priest Huitzil speaks to his people, saying that his death is near and that the gods are going to transform him and give his flesh to the god Tetzauhteotl, at which point he is converted and transformed into the god himself; thus his name: Huitzilopochtli Tetzauhteotl.

Thus, they begin the wandering to find their new place in the world indicated by their god. The people undergo many adventures during their peregrination. They settle in various places, and it is important to note how, from the time of leaving Aztlan, they were to pass through a place called

Cohualtepec and another called Chicomoztoc, meaning "seven caves." This is important because groups migrating prior to the Aztecs also mention these places in their migration stories. That is to say, the Aztecs are actually incorporating into their sacred histories the myths of other peoples, prior to or contemporary with their presence in Aztlan.

A point of interest during their wanderings is the presence of conflicts between the god Huitzilopochtli and feminine personalities. It is said that the larger group separated from one of the groups led by Malinalxochitl, sister of Huitzilopochtli and one to whom black arts and witchcraft are attributed. Later there will be a new confrontation and disputes with another woman, Coyolxauhqui, also

Scene depicting the Aztecs leaving their mythical home of Aztlan, from the *Codex Boturini,* Museo Nacional de Antropología, México, D.F.

a relative of the god. She heads the group or clan of the Huitznahua. The importance that this confrontation will have for the Mexica is so great that it is worth closer examination.

THE MYTH OF COATEPEC

There is a moment in the journey that is very important for the clans that will make up the Aztec group. That is when they arrive at Coatepec (Hill of the Serpent) and decide to settle there. With their knowledge of water, they build a dam and begin to produce a whole series of aquatic products, such as shrimp, fish, various plants, and birds. The place begins to prosper, and the people from the clan of Huitznahua, who were part of the larger group from the beginning of the pilgrimage, decide that this is the place indicated for them to remain for good. Nevertheless, the god Huitzilopochtli (or the people from the clan of Huitzilopochtli) does not agree, and he becomes furious at the Huitznahua. Durán's chronicle relates the following words from the Huitznahua:

> "Here is the place where you are to achieve glory and the exaltation of your name, this is the head of your kingdom; order your parents and grandparents to confer about it and let there be an end to

the wandering in search of more peace than we have here, so that the Aztecs and Mexicans may rest here and their work can have end." Angered, the god Huitzilopochtli responded to the priests and said: "Who are those who wish to change my determination and object and put an end to them? Are they by chance greater than I? Tell them that I will seek revenge before tomorrow, so that they dare not give an opinion about what I have already decided and for which I was sent, and so that they all will know that they are to obey only me."[2]

The chronicle continues, relating how at midnight a great noise was heard and on the next day the principals were found dead (along with their leader, a woman named Coyolxauhqui), all with their chests open and hearts removed. It is worth noting that this style of death, or sacrifice, is destined for, among others, those who are captured in battle.

This act, which serves to reinforce the god's (or his group's) power, is very important, as is the fact that Coatepec, the site of this conflict, is located near Tula, the Toltec capital city. What is all this saying to us? There is no doubt that some important social transformation occurs at that place. And certainly it is related to an act of war, of combat. It may be that this sacred history tells of a revolt undertaken against the Toltec oppressor

Coyolxauhqui head. Greenstone sculpture, Museo Nacional de Antropología, México, D.F. *(Height: 28 inches.)*

with the aid of other similarly subjugated tributaries that culminates in the destruction of Tula; or there could have been internal differences between the clan of Huitznahua and that of Huitzilopochtli, where the latter prevails and crushes the uprising. Either way, this event is of great importance for the Aztecs, so great that the historical war of mortals becomes a mythical war of deities in their memory. Another important fact is that the myth speaks to us of the birth of the god Huitzilopochtli, despite the fact that, as we have seen, the god existed before that. We might think that the triumph obtained in the war, either against the Toltecs or internally through conflicts with another clan, will be the basis for indicating the destiny of the god, a warrior god, born to fight and destroy his enemies. So the destiny of the Aztec people is also to accompany into battle their principal god, the god of the sun and of war, Huitzilopochtli.

What follows is the myth about the event that has been left to us, based upon the *Florentine Codex* and a Spanish translation by Miguel León-Portilla:

On Coatepec, in the direction of Tula,
a woman had been living,
a woman dwelt there
by the name of Coatlicue.

She was the mother of the four hundred
    Southerners,
and a sister of one of them
named Coyolxauhqui.

And this Coatlicue was doing penance there,
she would sweep, she was in charge of sweeping,
and so she did her penance,
on Coatepec, the Mountain of the Serpent.

And once
as Coatlicue was sweeping
some plumage fell on her,
like a ball of fine feathers.

Coatlicue picked it up at once,
she put it in her bosom.

When she had finished sweeping,
she looked for the feather which she had put in
    her bosom,
but she saw nothing there.

From that moment Coatlicue was pregnant.
When the four hundred Southerners saw
that their mother was pregnant,
they became very angry; they said:

"Who has done this to you?
Who has made you pregnant?
He has insulted us, he has dishonored us."

And their sister Coyolxauhqui
said to them:

"Brothers, she has dishonored us,
we must kill our mother,
the depraved woman who now is pregnant.
Who made what she carries in her bosom?"

When Coatlicue discovered this,
she was very frightened,
she was very saddened.
But her son Huitzilopochtli, who was in her bosom,
comforted her, said to her:

"Don't be afraid.
I know what I must do."

Coatlicue, having heard
the words of her son,
took great comfort,
her heart was calmed,
she felt tranquil.

And meanwhile, the four hundred Southerners
gathered to take council,
and unanimously they agreed
to kill their mother
because she had disgraced them.

They were very angry,
they were very agitated,
as if their hearts were going to leave their bodies.

Coatlicue, Aztec earth goddess. Stone sculpture from the Museo Nacional de Antropología, México, D.F. *(Height: 45 inches.)*

Coyolxauhqui greatly incited them,
inflamed her brothers' anger,
so they would kill their mother.

And the four hundred Southerners
were like captains,
they twisted and snarled their hair
as warriors fix their hair.

But one named Cuahuitlicac
was false in his words.

What the four hundred Southerners said,
he went to tell it at once,
he went to reveal it to Huitzilopochtli.

And Huitzilopochtli answered:

"Be careful, be alert,
my uncle, I know well what I must do."

And when finally they had agreed,
when the four hundred Southerners were resolved
to kill, to destroy their mother,
then they began to move out,
Coyolxauhqui guided them.

They felt very strong, adorned,
decorated for war,
they distributed among themselves their vestments
    of paper,
their destiny, their nettles,
the painted stripes of paper hanging on them,
they tied little bells on the calves of their legs,
the little bells called *oyohualli.*

Their arrows had sharp points.

Then they began to move out,
they went in order, in a row,
in an orderly squadron,
Coyolxauhqui guided them.

But Cuahuitlicac at once went up to the mountain
to speak from there to Huitzilopochtli,
he said to him:
"They're coming now."

Huitzilopochtli answered him:
"Look carefully at where they are."

Then Cuahuitlicac said:
"Now they're passing through Tzompantitlan."

And once more Huitzilopochtli said to him:
"Where are they now?"

Cuahuitlicac answered him:
"Now they are passing through Caxalpan."

And again Huitzilopochtli asked Cuahuitlicac:
"Look carefully at where they are."

At once Cuahuitlicac answered him:
"Now they are coming up the side of the mountain."

And yet once more Huitzilopochtli said to him:
"Look carefully where they are."

Then Cuahuitlicac said to him:
"Now they are on the mountain top, they are
    drawing near,
Coyolxauhqui is guiding them."

At that moment Huitzilopochtli was born,
he dressed himself in his finery,
his shield of eagle feathers,
his darts, his blue dart thrower,
the notable turquoise dart thrower.

He painted his face
with diagonal stripes,
with the color called "child's paint."

On his head he placed fine feathers,
he put on his earplugs.

And on one of his feet, the left one was very thin,
he wore a sandal covered with feathers,
and his two legs and his two arms
he had them painted blue.

And the one named Tochancalqui
took out the serpent made of candlewood,
whose name was Xiuhcoatl,
who obeyed Huitzilopochtli.

Then with it he wounded Coyolxauhqui,
he cut off her head,
which was left abandoned
on the slope of Coatepetl.

Coatlicue giving birth to Huitzilopochtli, from the *Florentine Codex,* sixteenth-century colonial manuscript compiled by Fray Bernardino de Sahagún (México: Secretaria de Gobernación, 1979 fascimile edition).

Huitzilopochtli and Coyolxauhqui, from the *Florentine Codex,* sixteenth-century colonial manuscript compiled by Fray Bernardino de Sahagún (México: Secretaria de Gobernación, 1979 fascimile edition).

The body of Coyolxauhqui
rolled down the slope,
it fell apart in pieces,
her hands, her legs, her torso
fell in different places.

Then Huitzilopochtli raised up,
he pursued the four hundred Southerners,
he kept on pursuing them, he scattered them
from the top of Coatepetl,
the Mountain of the Serpent.

And when he had followed them
to the foot of the mountain,
he pursued them, he chased them like rabbits,
around the mountain.

Four times he chased them around.

In vain they tried to do something against him,
in vain they turned and faced him,
to the sound of their bells,
and they slapped their shields.

They could do nothing,
they could achieve nothing,
they could defend themselves with nothing.

Huitzilopochtli pursued them, he chased them,
he destroyed them, he annihilated them, he
    obliterated them.

And then he left them,
he kept on pursuing them.

But they begged him often, they said to him:
"Enough! Enough!"

But Huitzilopochtli was not satisfied with this,
with force he wrathfully attacked them,
pursued them.

Only a few could escape his presence,
could free themselves from his hands.

They went toward the south,
because they went toward the south
they are called Southerners,
those few who escaped
from the hands of Huitzilopochtli.

And when Huitzilopochtli had killed them,
when he had expressed his anger,
he took from them their finery, their adornments,
their destiny, put them on, appropriated them,
incorporated them into his destiny,
made them his own insignia.

And this Huitzilopochtli, as people said,
was a portent,
because from a single feather
which fell into the womb of his mother, Coatlicue,
he was conceived.

No one ever appeared as his father.

The Mexicas venerated him,
made sacrifices to him,
honored and served him.

And Huitzilopochtli paid back
those who behaved that way.

And his cult was taken from there,
from Coatepec, the Mountain of the Serpent,
as it was practiced from times
most ancient.[3]

The myth had at least two levels of meaning in the world of Moctezuma. It is the theological justification for the sanctification and support of war as an economic means of controlling the enemy. It also shows the supremacy of the sun god and his daily victory over the nocturnal powers represented by the moon (Coyolxauhqui) and the stars of the South (the *centzon huitznahua*). The weapon of Huitzilopochtli, the Xiuhcoatl, or fire serpent, we interpret as the ray of sun that appears in the morning to destroy the night. It is not unusual that an agricultural people of the sun would see in this daily event just one more of those cycles of life and death that throughout the year are also observed in the sharp contrasts between the rainy season and the dry season. It is, once more, the observation of the universe and its cyclical processes that forms the basis for a complete conceptualization of the universe.

Huitzilopochtli with fire serpent, from the *Florentine Codex,* sixteenth-century colonial manuscript compiled by Fray Bernardino de Sahagún (México: Secretaria de Gobernación, 1979 fascimile edition).

The Mexica migration passes by Coatepec, from the *Codex Boturini,* Museo Nacional de Antropología, México, D.F.

THE FOUNDING OF THE CITY OF TENOCHTITLAN

After these events, which occurred on Coatepec, the Aztecs continue their march southward. This part of the journey is easier to reconstruct, for the places that are mentioned can still be identified. In a sense, Coatepec is a watershed, with the prior events constituting mythical events, and those coming after Coatepec being more tangible. The war that took place on that site brings Aztec history into clearer focus. According to the chroniclers, the Aztecs pass through such places as Tula-Coatepec, Atitalaquia, and Atotonilco, until they come to penetrate some areas on the shores of Lake Texcoco, such as Tzompanco, Ecatepec, Pantitlan, and so forth. And they settle in Chapultepec (Grasshopper Hill), where they are to reside for many years. There they have problems with the neighboring peoples, who begin to harass them. They are forced, therefore, to resettle in the domain of Culhuacan, governed by Achitometl, who allows them to settle in Tizapan, a place full of snakes. Even so, the Aztecs survive and more; they ask Achitometl for a daughter to marry one of their own. The lord of Culhuacan agrees and thus establishes a marriage alliance that benefits the Mexica because it gives them legitimate access to the Toltec heritage. But at one of their festivities the Aztecs sacrifice the daughter of Achitometl, and a priest adorns himself with her flayed hide. The father has been invited to the ceremony and in the dark temple discovers that his daughter's skin is serving as the sacred costume of the priest. The indignation is great, and war is immediately unleashed between Culhuacan and the Aztecs, who are besieged and persecuted in the vicinity of the lake. They pass through such places as Acatzitzitlan and Mexicalcingo until arriving in an area under the control of the lord of Azcapotzalco, Tezozomoc. The latter, governor of the Tepaneca group, has great powers within the Valley, and various important cities are under his jurisdiction, including Coyoacan, governed by his son, Maxtla.

Tezozomoc of Azcapotzalco accepts the vassalage of the Aztecs and makes them tributaries. They are assigned some small island in the middle of the lake where they settle and found their city, having also to pay tribute in various products of the lake and to collaborate in the Lord of Azcapotzalco's wars. Thus, historical forces are

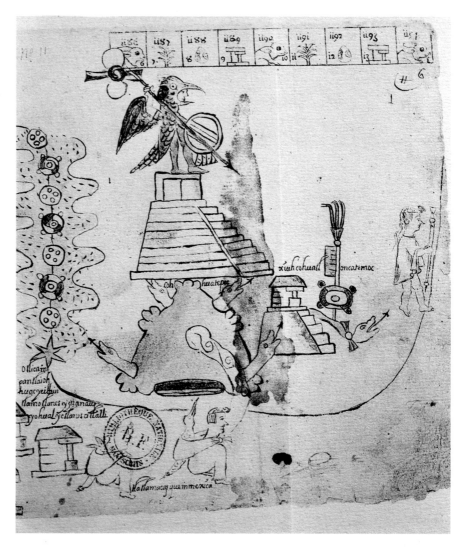

The Temple of Huitzilopochtli at Coatepec, from the *Codex Azcatitlan,* Bibliothèque Nationale, Paris, France.

dictating social experience: the Aztecs are obliged to settle in a place that is convenient to their Tepaneca oppressors, both strategically, because they are on the border with the Culhuacan domain, and also economically, because the lake products such as shrimp, fish, snakes, and various types of birds, among others, were necessities of the Azcapotzalcas. Equally necessary was their military participation with the Tepaneca forces in their expansionist drive. Nevertheless, the myth created by the Aztecs attempts to make the settlement in the middle of the lake seem to be the result of their arrival at the place chosen by their god. What does the myth tell us about this? We will

return again to Father Durán, sixteenth-century chronicler, where he relates this mythical event. The friar tells us that the first thing they found was a savine bush, all white,

> very beautiful, at the foot of which ran a spring. The second thing they saw was that all the willows that the spring had around it were white, without a single green leaf: all the cane in that place was white and also the reeds all around. There began to come out of the water all-white frogs and white fish and among them, some lovely white snakes. The water flowed out from between two large rocks, and it ran agreeably clear and pretty. The priests and elders, remembering what their god

17

The founding of Tenochtitlan, from the *Codex Durán,* Museo Nacional de Antropología, México, D.F.

had told them, began to cry with joy and pleasure, saying: "We have found the place that has been promised us; we have seen consolation and rest for the weary Mexican people; there is no more to be desired: be consoled, children and brothers, for what your god has promised you, we have now found and attained; because he told us that we would see fabulous things among the reed fields of this place where we were and wait for the commandment from our god, who will advise us of what we are to do."[4]

The following day they return to the same place and go a little farther, where they search for the sign of their god in the form of an eagle. The story says:

Seeing that there was no lack of mystery in all that, they moved ahead to search for the predicted eagle, and wandering from one place to another, they saw the cactus, and on top of it an eagle with its wings extended toward the rays of the sun, taking its heat in the coolness of the morning, and in its claws was a very elegant bird with precious and resplendent plumage. They, when they saw it, bowed down in reverence almost as [to] a divinity. The eagle, when he saw them, bowed down, lowering his head all around them. When they saw the eagle bow, they had seen what they wanted, and they began to cry and effuse and make ceremonies and visages and movements in signs of happiness and pleasure and showing their thanks, saying: "How did we merit so much good fortune? Who made us worthy of so much grace and greatness and excellence? We have seen what we wanted to see, we have attained what we were searching for, and we have found our city and site: thanks to the Lord of Creation and to our god Huitzilopochtli."[5]

Here we should indicate that the two days with different symbols signify something very important. On the first day they find everything related to white, which is taken from the myths of the mighty Toltecs, that is, it is a form of legitima-

Frontispiece depicting the founding of Tenochtitlan, *Codex Mendoza*.

tion of what is going to happen. Apparently, the Aztecs have incorporated Toltec symbols into their foundation myth in order to draw sacred authority into their city. On the following day they find the eagle on the cactus, that is, the symbol of their god Huitzilopochtli, god of the sun. In this way they sanctify the place in which they would establish the city.

The Aztecs immediately construct a small shrine to Huitzilopochtli and rejoice in this new sacred center they had set out to find years earlier when they left Aztlan. This place eventually becomes the most sacred enclave of the Aztec empire. In the middle of the sacred precinct of Tenochtitlan there will be the ceremonial area with the

Chimalpopoca, from page 5 of the *Codex Mendoza*.

Great Temple (the Templo Mayor) at the spot where the eagle was found; the area is marked off, separating it from the area where the houses will be located, the secular area. Plate 1 of the *Codex Mendoza* indicates the division the city will have, with its four major districts (which subsequently, with the development of the city, will become many more). Thus, in A.D. 1325, arises Tenochtitlan, the Aztec city, whose sacred precinct or ceremonial quarter with the Great Temple in its center is the umbilicus of their conception of the universe.

THE WAR OF LIBERATION

Settled in their city, the Aztecs dedicate themselves to the cultivation and exploitation of lake products. The control that Azcapotzalco has over them causes them to seek certain alliances to alleviate their subservience. They request a Tepaneca princess for their governor, Acamapichtli (A.D. 1375–1395), a marriage that gives birth to Chimalpopoca (A.D. 1417–1427), grandson, therefore, of the powerful ruler Tezozomoc of Azcapotzalco. This royal alliance is used to partially alleviate the burden of required tribute on Teno-

chtitlan. Nevertheless, the Tepaneca nobles do not approve of the Aztecs, and they try to impose even greater taxes on them. Apparently Maxtla, the ruler of Coyoacan, orders Chimalpopoca killed, and a political and military crisis develops when Tezozomoc dies at an advanced age. War erupts between Azcapotzalco and various cities allied against it. Texcoco and Tenochtitlan lead the rebellion, and after several battles in which victory shifts from one side to the other, Tenochtitlan finally prevails. One of the captains of the Aztec army is Moctezuma, who years later will assume the throne of the empire with the name Huehue Moctezuma, or Moctezuma I, the Elder. At the moment of triumph the military and political leader of the Aztecs is Itzcoatl, "Obsidian Serpent" (A.D. 1427–1440), who leads his people to victory and frees them from the Tepaneca yoke. This occurred in the year A.D. 1428.

The hate that has accumulated during so many years of vassalage pours forth at this point. Now Azcapotzalco is the one under the control of the Aztecs, to whom it must pay tribute. According to Durán, at the moment of triumph the Aztecs were relentless with the Tepanecas. Thus, the chronicler relates the event:

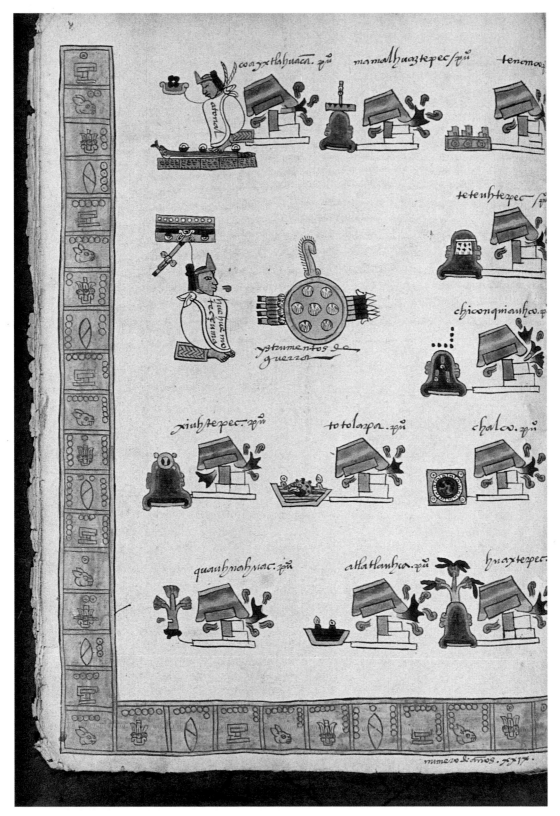

The conquest history of Moctezuma I as pictured in the *Codex Mendoza,* page 7, verso.

The Mexica, following their victory, like blood-thirsty dogs, full of fury and anger, followed them until they penetrated the hills, where the Azcapotzalcas, prostrate, surrendered their weapons, promising to give them lands and to build houses and plant fields, to be their perpetual tributaries, to give them stone, lime and wood, and whatever quantity they needed of corn, beans, sage, chile and all the vegetables and seeds they eat.[6]

After the victory over Azcapotzalco, the Triple Alliance is formed among Tenochtitlan, Texcoco, and Tacuba. This new political order begins the expansion of the Aztec empire in two phases — first within the Valley of Mexico and afterward outside it. The second Tepaneca city conquered is Coyoacan, which ends up similarly subservient to Tenochtitlan. From here they attack Xochimilco, a city of great importance because of its control over the areas of intensive cultivation. We should remember that the southern part of the lake was occupied by a population mostly dedicated to the cultivation of the system of chinampa. Thus, Xochimilco's strategic importance in agricultural production made it a coveted prey for the victorious Aztec armies.

Under Itzcoatl's aggressive leadership, the Triple Alliance secured control in the vicinity of the lake and initiated expansion into other regions. The northern part of the current state of Guerrero was conquered and the initial outline of the Aztec empire was consolidated. At his death he was succeeded on the throne by Moctezuma I (A.D. 1440–1469), beginning a period in which the Aztecs and their allies reached distant regions of Mesoamerica.

As we see, the victory over Azcapotzalco marked the beginning of liberation and expansion. The time between the founding of the city of Tenochtitlan in A.D. 1325 and its emancipation in 1428 was over a hundred years, that is, a hundred years during which the Aztecs were tributaries and subjects of exploitation by the Azcapotzalcas. They needed almost another hundred years, from A.D. 1428 to 1521, to achieve their unprecedented pinnacle of power and to take control of a large part of Mesoamerica. Thus, the people of Huitzilopochtli lived their destiny of misery and glory. How was this society organized on the eve of the arrival of the Spaniards? What of their education, their ritual and social specialists, their trade, in short, their most essential characteristics?

SOCIAL AND ECONOMIC ORGANIZATION

Aztec society was deeply divided into two large groups: the *pipiltin* and the *macehualtin*. The pipiltin made up the governing group including the nobles, who occupied the principal positions, both civil and religious. Control of all things social was in their hands, and both the ideological apparatus (religion and control of knowledge) as well as the military apparatus (the army) had commanders from the Aztec elite. The commander in chief and head of state was the *tlatoani,* elected from among the nobility, whose position was not hereditary. One of the required characteristics for the position was a profound knowledge of the sacred forces of the cosmos and another was an outstanding career in the wars of expansion; thus, when he assumed power he would combine the great priest and great military captain in his person. Tlatoani means "he who speaks," "he who has the facility of speech." He was required to do two things besides govern his people: enlarge the temple of his god Huitzilopochtli and expand the power of the empire.

An entire administrative apparatus supported the tlatoani. Conquered regions had a *calpixque,* or local administrator, who was in control of the tribute the conquered peoples had to pay periodically to Tenochtitlan. Internally there was the *calpuleque,* chief of a *calpulli,* or type of "clan" that made up the many neighborhoods of Tenochtitlan. These clans had their own lands and provided men for communal work within the city and also contingents of warriors when needed for conquests. The *tetecuhtin* were also from the nobility, and one arrived at that rank by excelling in war, which led to the possession of lands and those who worked them. In general, we can say that the nobility, or *pipiltin,* enjoyed the following exclusive privileges:

- Only the nobles could have their own land
- They were given preference for public positions
- They were not obliged to work the land
- They did not pay tribute
- There were courts exclusively for them
- They could have more than one wife
- They had exclusive use of certain insignia
- They studied in a special school called *calmecac*

A young man goes to war, holding a spear and carrying arrows, a shield, and his belongings, page 63 of the *Codex Mendoza.*

As we see, the privileges were significant, especially freedom from tribute payments to the state and education in schools where they were prepared to be priests, warriors, and governors. This school played an important role, for there was a rigid apprenticeship that made of the Aztec noble an individual prepared for whatever position he might choose.

On the other hand, the group of macehualtin, or common people, included the major part of the population. They belonged to one of the calpulli (clan) and were farm workers, potters, goldsmiths, construction workers, carpenters, weavers, fishermen, lapidaries, in short, a whole range of artisans and specialists who lived from the exchange of their products. Unlike the nobles, the *macehualtin* had to pay tribute to the tlatoani in two ways: with part of their product and by participating in communal works through their calpulli, work done by

groups of twenty to a hundred men under the supervision of a "boss." These were actually public works projects. In addition, the macehuales were prepared for war, that is, they were soldiers who formed the Aztec army as part of their calpulli. As can be seen, the organization of these clans was the basic element in the organization of the city. In each of them was a school called *tepochcalli* where one learned arts and crafts in addition to military routine.

There was a social group called *mayeque* who worked other people's land and paid a tax to the owner. There were also slaves, although it must be noted that they were not slaves in the same sense as, for example, those of ancient Rome. One could become a slave for nonpayment of a debt or for betting and losing on a ball game. The commission of a robbery or a murder caused the guilty one to become a slave of the victim or his family. Some-

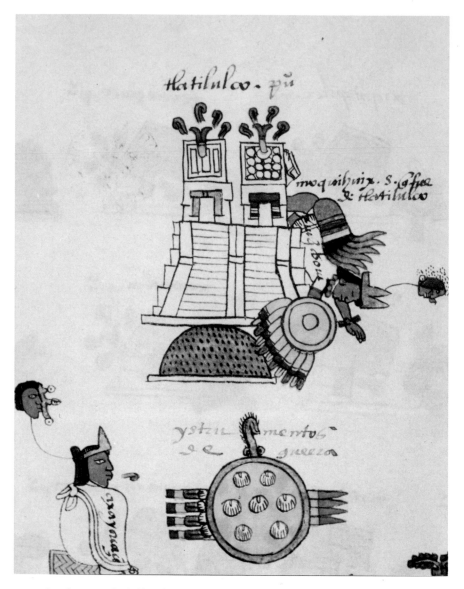

Hatilulco · pu

moquihuix · S · (affea
& Hatilulco

ystrumentus
de guezos

The death of Moquihuix and the conquest of Tlatelolco during the reign of Axayacatl, *Codex Mendoza,* page 10.

one in financial difficulty could sell himself as a slave. However, a slave could regain his or her liberty by paying the debt or taking refuge in a temple. A female slave was freed if the master took her as a wife. Offspring of a slave did not inherit the status, and slavery as a practice did not figure importantly in the Aztec economy as it did in Western culture.

Another important group were the tradesmen or *pochteca.* They steadily gained status in Aztec society and, although they had to pay taxes to the tlatoani, their work as travelers to distant areas permitted them to provide the empire with espio-

nage services. This role was of prime importance because, under the pretext of trading activities, they disguised themselves and penetrated into the still-unconquered provinces and reported all they saw to Tenochtitlan. A sixteenth-century chronicler speaks of the entry of the tradesmen into Tzinacatlan: "When the tradesmen entered Tzinacatlan, it was still not conquered: when they entered it was not apparent that they were Mexicans because they were disguised and looked like the locals. They wore their hair like the inhabitants of Tzinacatlan . . . they tried to imitate them in every way and they learned their language. So they

People working with chinampas, and corn deity in the background. Mural painted in 1942 by Diego Rivera at the Palacio Nacional, México D.F.

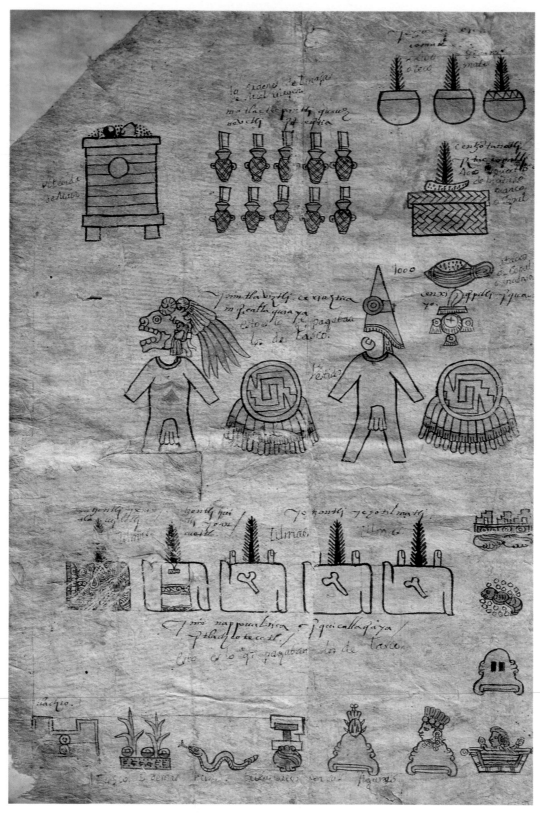

A page from the *Matrícula de Tributos* depicting products paid to Tenochtitlan as tribute. Museo Nacional de Antropología, México, D.F.

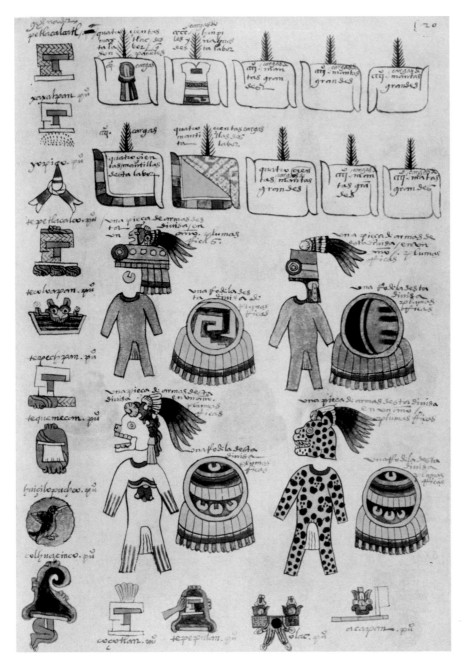

Tribute items paid by communities to Tenochtitlan, page 20 of the *Codex Mendoza*.

entered incognito, such that absolutely no one realized they were Mexicans."[7]

The tradesmen's importance also resided in the fact that many of the products they traded belonged to the government. They enjoyed certain privileges such as having a personal militia that accompanied them on their travels. They could also declare war in their own name. Within the marketplace they had their own judges who handed down sentences in cases of commercial disputes, among others.

Speaking of the market, the principal one was established in the city of Tlatclolco, neighbor of Tenochtitlan. This city was created a few years after the settlement of the first Aztec city, around A.D. 1337, on an island slightly to the north of Tenochtitlan. Although they were members of the same ethnic group, the Tlatelolcans acted independently

Tlaloc, the rain god. Copal resin sculpture, Museo Nacional de Antropología, México, D.F. *(Height: 12 inches.)*

ity these chinampa fields were very fertile. The chinampas extended all along the southern edge of the lake and resulted in enormous production. Planting was done with traditional tools like the *coa,* or wooden planting stick, and farmers also used a type of shovel. A large number of people must have dedicated themselves to the care of the crops. The most common products were corn, beans, tomatoes, squash, and chile peppers, all known in Mesoamerica for several thousand years.

As far as war and the taxes it produced, it is sufficient to point out that around the time of the arrival of the Spaniards, some 371 tribes from thirty-three provinces in different areas of Mesoamerica paid tribute to the Aztecs. Two important sources speak to us of the conquered peoples: the *Matrícula de Tributos* and the *Codex Mendoza.* In these sources it can be seen how each town periodically delivered to the Aztecs the tribute that corresponded to what was produced in its region. Thus, there were taxes in the form of loads of corn, squash, cacao, honey, beans, and other foodstuffs; in raw materials such as semiprecious stones, copal, lime for building, and other products such as bird feathers, cotton warrior costumes, and animal skins. In short, the Aztec city and the tlatoani's coffers were filled with products that originated in the different subjugated regions. Dr. Pedro Carrasco has said of tribute: "The greatest accumulation of goods in the royal warehouses in Mexico probably arrived as tribute from the subject provinces; thus the enormous importance of war as a means of sustaining and increasing the economic base of the large political centers."[8]

from the first city of the Aztecs and developed an inclination toward commercial activity. In the year A.D. 1473, under the government of Axayacatl (A.D. 1469–1481), conflict broke out between the two cities. Tlatelolco was defeated; its governor, Moquihuix, was killed; and it was incorporated into Tenochtitlan. The competition between the two cities may well have been due to the high economic level achieved by Tlatelolco, a central point for all commercial products and where the distribution system that so impressed the Spaniards was located.

So, the basis of the Aztec economy consisted of two large activities: (1) agricultural production and (2) war as a means of imposing taxes on the conquered peoples. In the case of agriculture, high-productivity techniques called chinampas had been developed to exploit very wet areas where canals were dug, and the mud from them was piled in ridges. Thanks to the constant humid-

An interesting point is worth noting here. The Aztec need for agriculture and war were both present in the main temple, dedicated to Tlaloc, the god of rain, fertility, and the growth of plants, and to Huitzilopochtli, warrior god and god of conquest. Thus, the Aztecs established this relationship with their gods out of the necessities of their own subsistence.

COSMOVISION

All peoples have their own image of the universe. The Aztecs of central Mexico inherited a concept of the universe that came from the remote past, when cities like Teotihuacan were developed in the first seven centuries A.D. What was the structure of the universe for them? What position did the gods and mortals have within it? What was their vision of the birth of the sun, of the earth, of humankind? The answers to all these questions are encompassed in the term *cosmovision,* which is related closely to different types of myths, to religion versus rituals, and to a philosophy manifested in a people's concept of the structure and rhythm of the universe.

Let us begin with this last point. The key to understanding this mode of thought is to grasp the concept of duality. The pre-Columbian peoples of Mesoamerica were constant observers of nature. The movement of the stars, the day and the night, the change from a rainy season to a dry season in the course of a year, the birth and death of plants and of humans themselves, were cyclical phenomena that did not pass unnoticed. Thus, these dualities were present in all thinking about the universe and were manifested in some of the primordial myths.

Some of these myths speak of the primordial couple Tonacatecuhtli and Tonacacihuatl, a duality that dwells in the highest level of the cosmos. They were also called Omecihuatl and Ometecuhtli, the Lord and Lady of Duality. They create four gods (the three Tezcatlipocas and Quetzalcoatl), who with their struggles and alternations create the four Ages, or Suns, and try to make human life better and better along with the food that sustains it.

Each of these gods occupies a superior place in the universe. They create the first human couple, Cipactonal and Oxomoco, and give them the skills of planting and weaving. A very important part of

this myth shows that these gods determine the structure of the universe and create the calendar. The story goes like this:

> Then they made the days and divided them into months, giving each month twenty days, and so they made Mictlantecuhtli and Mictecacihuatl, husband and wife, and these were the gods of the underworld and they put them there. Then they created the heavens, beyond the thirteenth, and they made the water and in it they created a large fish called Cipactli, which is like an alligator, and from this fish they made the earth.[9]

The action of the gods, as can be seen, resulted in the creation of the solar calendar of 360 days plus five "hollow" or unlucky days, important for agricultural people such as the Aztecs. The calendar was based on two great cycles, the dry season and the rainy one, divided by festivities in honor of the god of fire. It was organized by the observation of the movement of the sun — equinoxes and solstices — in relation to the rainy season when all was born and the dry season when everything died. There was also the ritual calendar of 260 days, which is thought to be related to the time of human gestation and the lunar cycles. We could say that the solar calendar is masculine and the ritual calendar is feminine.

The structure of the universe is also the work of these gods. The myths speak of the levels of the underworld, of the celestial levels, and of the earth as an intermediate level between those two. Let us look at each of these levels.

The Earthly Level
The earth was created from the body of a cipactli, or a type of crocodile. It is the place inhabited by humans and has a center or navel that is united with the higher or celestial level where the stars are found and where certain divine events occur, as well as with the underworld or place of the dead. This fundamental center is formed by the

The celestial levels in Aztec cosmology, from the *Codex Vaticanus 3738 A* (Academische Druck und Verlagsanstalt, Graz, Austria, 1979 facsimile edition).

Great Temple, from where, in turn, originate the four directions of the universe. Recall that the Great Temple is the principal building of the ceremonial area of Tenochtitlan within which there are seventy-eight ritual buildings, according to Sahagún. Causeways lead to this sacred precinct, each oriented to a cardinal point: one from Tacuba to the west; one from Tepeyac toward the north; and one from Iztapalapa toward the south. In some histories a fourth causeway, to the east, is mentioned — one that must not have been very long because the lake comes very close to the ceremonial center on that side.

The Celestial Level

The celestial level is conceived as moving upward from the earth in a series of tiers. Having

knowledge of the movement of the stars and of phenomena such as rain, the comets, and lightning bolts, the Mexicas created the various levels of the heavens in their cosmovision.

To begin, we point out that there are references to nine levels, although at times eleven and thirteen are spoken of also. It is important to note that these nine celestial levels correspond and are related to the nine stages of the underworld. Evidence exists of the characteristics of each of these levels. In the *Codex Vaticanus 3738 A* we see that the first level corresponds to the moon and the clouds. The second is where the stars are found; it was known as *citlalco*. The third level is where the sun crosses daily from east to west. In the fourth is found Venus, and there is another source that tells us that this level is related to the sister of the Tlaloques, Huixtocihuatl, deity of salt water. The fifth level is the one through which comets pass and where celestial rotation is manifest. The sixth

The earthly level and the levels of the underworld in Aztec cosmology, from the *Codex Vaticanus 3738 A* (Academische Druck und Verlagsanstalt, Graz, Austria, 1979 facsimile edition).

Mictecacihuatl, goddess of the underworld. Stone sculpture, Museo Nacional de Antropología, México, D.F. *(Height: 30 inches.)*

Mictecacihuatl, goddess of the dead. Stone sculpture, Museo Nacional de Antropología, México, D.F. *(Height: 48 inches.)*

Giant serpent heads, from the base of the Great Temple of Tenochtitlan. Museo del Templo Mayor, México, D.F.

and seventh are represented by colors, while the eighth is considered the one where storms are formed or the place with corners of obsidian stones. From the ninth up are the levels where the more powerful gods resided, with the last two corresponding to the "place of duality," Omeyocan.

As can be seen, there is a clear relationship between some of these levels or stages and the patterned movement and observation of natural and astronomical phenomena.

The Underworld Level

The underworld is conceived as going from the earth downward, even though we have already spoken of how the North is related to *mictlampa*, or the place of the dead. Although further in-depth

Tlaloc, the rain god. Greenstone sculpture with shell and pyrite inlays, Museo del Templo Mayor, México, D.F. *(Height: 8 inches.)*

social and cosmic structure. Thus, one would go to Tlalocan if one died from some water-related illness, or would go to accompany the sun if one died as a consequence of war (sacrificed as a captive or in combat). On the other hand, those who died a natural death went to Mictlan, to which one arrived after passing through eight places, staving off diverse ambushes and difficulties, to end up deposited in the ninth stage, where dwelled the gods of death, Mictlantecuhtli and Mictecacihuatl. It is significant that the vertical elements that we have seen in the celestial realm, which culminate in the place of duality, Omeyocan, have their equivalents and balancing elements in the underworld, where this duality created by the gods also resides.

Both Sahagún and the *Codex Vaticanus 3738 A* make reference to the places one had to pass through in order to arrive at Mictlan. For the cleric, the first step was to cross a river and two hills that touch each other. Then followed the place of the snake that guards the road, the place of the green lizard, the place of the eight wildernesses, crossing eight passes, the place of razor-cold wind, crossing the Chiconahuapan River, and, finally, arrival at Mictlan. The other version begins with the place where the corpse, which will be eaten by Tlaltecuhtli, is deposited in the earth. From there the soul crosses a river (pass of the water); then it was necessary to traverse the place where the hills are found, then follow the obsidian hill, the place with the people shot with arrows, the place where hearts are eaten, the place of obsidian wind of the dead, and the place without exit for smoke.

The two versions have similarities and differences, although it is well to understand that some concepts have their equivalences in the other. Such is the case of the razor-cold wind, on the one hand, and the place of the obsidian wind on the other. It is possible that the reference to the place without an exit for smoke corresponds to Mictlan, for the

study of the topic is still needed, we will analyze in what follows the nine stages that composed the lower level, the underworld.

Before looking at the journey that the individual made when he died, or more properly that his soul (*teyolia,* in Nahuatl) made, we should again make clear that it was the form of death that determined where the individual would go after death. These determinations were important within an agrarian-warrior society, so the places of the dead were closely tied to those two economic aspects that sustained the whole Mexica

Huehueteotl, the old god of fire. Stone sculpture found to the north of the Great Temple of Tenochtitlan, Museo del Templo Mayor, México, D.F. *(Height: 26 inches.)*

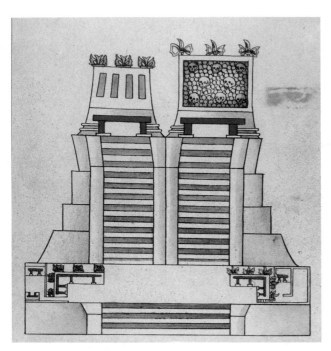

The Great Temple of Tenochtitlan, from the *Codex Durán,*
Museo Nacional de Antropología, México, D.F.

latter is always referred to as a place without light or windows, a place of great darkness, without an exit to the street, and so forth.

Besides this vertical structure of the cosmos, the horizontal structure consisted of the four directions of the universe. Each of them was ruled by a god, a color, a symbol, and a tree. Representations like that in the *Codex Féjérváry-Mayer* indicate this division in the form of a flower with four petals. We know that, in general, the south side of the universe corresponded to the blue Tezcatlipoca, who was none other than Huitzilopochtli, their protector. His symbol was the rabbit (*tochtli,* in Nahuatl). The east corresponded to one of the Tezcatlipocas also identified with Xipe Totec. His color was red and his symbol was the *acatl,* or reed. The north belonged to the black Tezcatlipoca and its symbol was the sacrificial knife, the *tecpatl.* It was related to death; it was in the direction of mictlampa. The west corresponded to Quetzalcoatl, its color was white, and

its symbol was the *calli,* or house of the sun. It was related to the direction of women, the *cihuatlampa.*

All these levels and directions were oriented by one powerful place. The main center where the upper and lower levels intersected and where the four directions of the universe originated was the Great Temple of Tenochtitlan. It was the most sacred place, and all these levels crossed there. In its actual architecture the building was a summary of its cosmogonic concept. The general platform that supports the building represents the earthly level. The excavations of 1978–1982 found the greatest number of offerings dedicated to their gods in this platform. The four superimposed, pyramidal bodies are four more-celestial levels that culminate in the dual concept of the two shrines of Tlaloc and Huitzilopochtli on the upper platform. Through the Great Temple one can descend to the levels of the underworld. We saw that one of the first steps toward Mictlan is the traversal of two touching hills. This is represented in the two hills, Coatepec and Tonacatepetl, that are present in the Great Temple. The first is dedicated to Huitzilopochtli and is a reactualization of the combat that occurred on Coatepec and of the importance that the event had for the Aztecs. The other hill is related to Tlaloc, inside of which was kept the Aztecs' rudimentary sustenance, corn.

So this cosmovision had a material form, a center of centers, given shape in the Great Temple. And as a fundamental center, in it was contained the sacred presence Ometeotl, the dual first principle, identified in the old god of fire, Xiuhtecuhtli-Huehueteotl. There is an ancient song that describes this god at the center of the universe. He guards the equilibrium of the universe and inhabits both the heavenly levels and the underworld, but his place is the center of centers, the Great Temple. Here is the account: "Mother of the gods, father of the gods, the old god, stretched out on the navel of the earth, in an enclosure of turquoise

Eagle head from the Huitzilopochtli side of the Great Temple of Tenochtitlan, Museo del Templo Mayor, México, D.F.

Sculpted frogs from the Tlaloc side of the Great Temple of Tenochtitlan, Museo del Templo Mayor, México, D.F.

stones. He who is in the bluebird-colored waters, he who is enclosed in clouds, the old god, he who inhabits the shadows of the region of the dead, the lord of fire and of the year."[10] Various offerings dedicated to this deity were found in the Great Temple. He is depicted in the form of a toothless old man on his haunches, with a headband from which a bird springs. His presence is not surprising because he occupies his destined place: the center of universal order.

As we have seen, the whole idea of the universe starts with the observation of nature. Pre-Columbian peoples lived immersed in a changing world, and their myths sprang forth from the appreciation of these cycles that are manifested through struggles among the gods themselves. The Great Temple expresses that constant fundamental duality. The Tlaloc side is that of fertility, of water, of the growth of plants, in short, everything related to life. On the other hand, the Huitzilopochtli side is related to sacrifice, war, and death. There abides the myth of the daily struggle of the sun (Huitzilopochtli) against the moon and the stars (Coyolxauhqui and the four hundred Southerners). It is the presence of life and death in the main Aztec temple.

ARTISTIC EXPRESSION

Humans in all periods have been the preeminent creators. So it is that in any circumstance and at any level of development through which humanity has passed, people have created tools, both to satisfy our material necessities as well as to allow for artistic expression that allows us to grasp nature and transform it through stone, murals, clay, the word, and through space itself. Each society can identify itself through those expressions, and they acquire their own characteristic style.

We can now approach the expression of a people such as the Aztecs. The first point to emphasize is the symbolic character of Aztec art. In fact, to understand pre-Columbian art, it is necessary to understand the society that produced it and how the symbolism is impressed upon it. Sculpture, painting, architecture, dance, and poetry all show the presence of religious symbolism. Scholars of the ancient art of Mexico have stated that pre-Columbian art begins and ends with myth and that there are two basic categories in this art: the terrible and the sublime.

The best-known artistic manifestation of the Aztec world is in sculpture. This is because archaeological discoveries emphasize this kind of work. In fact, between 1790, when the monumental sculptures of Coatlicue and the Calendar Stone were found in the main plaza of Mexico City, and February 21, 1978, when the statue of Coyolxauhqui and the subsequent discoveries of the Great Temple Project were made, we have uncovered an abundance of both major and minor sculpture produced by these people. These works, all sculpted with other stones, display a creative range of theme, craft, and style. It is impressive how at the same time they were sculpting the previously mentioned works — stone manifestations of their fantastic cosmogonic thought — they were also creating a figure like the Coyolxauhqui Stone, where the realism and movement of the figure represent the union of history and myth. The same attention to realism and cosmology occurs with the eagle found in 1985 in front of the Great Temple, where the anonymous artist who made it managed to fix the symbolic bird in stone down to the last detail. At the same time, the enormous head of Xiuhcoatl, the fire serpent, has a form that passes the limits of realism and approaches an abstraction akin to the fantastic. This brilliant dexterity is characteristic of Aztec art in particular and Mesoamerican art in general: the artist can create a spectacular synthesis in a figure or playfully concentrate on the tiniest detail from nature. Historical study of Aztec sculpture shows that there are not periods for the creation of certain

Detail of the Coyolxauhqui Stone, Museo del Templo Mayor, México, D.F.

Xiuhcoatl, the fire serpent, Museo Nacional de Antropología, México, D.F. *(Height: 38 inches.)*

styles of work. They are all made at the same time and are present simultaneously to the spectator.

It is significant that some Aztec sculptures, unlike Western art, where all the work done to a piece is meant to be seen, were carved underneath. Examples include the great statue of Coatlicue with the representation of Tlaltecuhtli, a deity that was carved underneath, that is, unseen. When León y Gama and, later, Alexander von Humboldt studied the goddess Coatlicue in the late eighteenth and early nineteenth centuries, they thought that she must have been located in a high place so the carving on the bottom could be seen. They did not understand that the figure carved there was an earthly god — the lord of the earth — who because of his attributes should be underneath. For the Westerner, all the work is to be seen. It is a dialogue between humans. For the Aztec in ancient Mexico, it had another character — it was a dialogue with the gods.

We could say much more about their sculpture. Suffice it to say that the subjects are quite varied. We have, for example, sculptures of animals. We have coiled snakes, different species of birds, jaguars, coyotes, turtles, and even masterfully executed insects. Such is the case with grasshoppers, among

Coatlicue (Woman with the Serpent Skirt). Monumental stone sculpture of the Aztec earth goddess, Museo Nacional de Antropología, México, D.F. *(Height: 115 inches.)*

Tlaltecuhtli, lord of the earth. Circular stone sculpture depicting the descending earth monster, Museo Nacional de Antropología, México, D.F. *(Diameter: 37 inches.)*

Tlaltecuhtli, the earth monster. Stone sculpture, Museo Nacional de Antropología, México, D.F. *(Height: 26 inches.)*

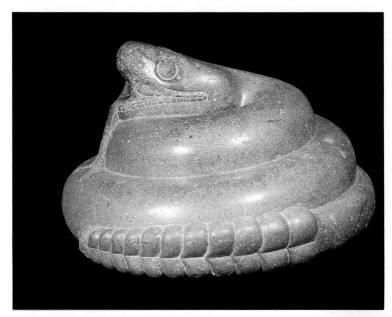

Coiled rattlesnake. Greenstone sculpture, Museo Nacional de Antropología, México, D.F. *(Diameter: 30 inches; height: 7 inches.)*

Coiled serpent. Stone sculpture, Museo Nacional de Antropología, México, D.F. *(Diameter: 34 inches; height: 5 inches.)*

Coiled serpent. Stone sculpture, Museo Nacional de Antropología, México, D.F. *(Height: 24 inches.)*

Eagle head. Polychromed stone sculpture, Museo del Templo Mayor, México, D.F. *(Height: 16 inches.)*

Eagle Cuauhxicalli. Basalt sculpture from the Great Temple of Tenochtitlan, Museo del Templo Mayor, México, D.F. *(55 x 32 x 28 inches.)*

Jaguar with speech glyph. Stone relief from El Cerro de Santa Cruz, Acalpixtla.

Stone sculpture in bas-relief with jaguar shown in profile, Museo Nacional de Antropología, México, D.F. *(26 x 26 inches.)*

Seated plumed coyote. Stone sculpture, Museo Nacional de Antropología, México, D.F. *(Height: 18 inches.)*

Feathered coyote. Stone sculpture, Museo Nacional de Antropología, México, D.F. *(Height: 18 inches.)*

Reclining feathered coyote. Stone sculpture, Museo Nacional de Antropología, México, D.F. *(Height: 11 inches.)*

Monkey or personage wearing Ehe-catl mask. Stone sculpture, Museo Nacional de Antropología, México, D.F. *(Height: 24 inches.)*

Macuilxochitl, Aztec god of music, represented as a turtle. Museo Nacional de Antropología, México, D.F. *(Height: 15 inches.)*

Stone sculpture depicting a squash, Museo Nacional de Antropología, México, D.F. *(Length: 12 inches.)*

Red stone sculpture depicting a grasshopper, Museo Nacional de Antropología, México, D.F. *(Length: 19 inches.)*

Standing man. Stone sculpture, Museo Nacional de Antropología, México, D.F. *(Height: 26 inches.)*

Head of a Mexica. Andesite sculpture with shell inlays, Museo Nacional de Antropología, México, D.F. *(Height: 7.5 inches.)*

Head of a Mexica. Andesite sculpture with obsidian and shell inlays, Museo Nacional de Antropología, México, D.F. *(Height: 7.5 inches.)*

Standing man. Stone sculpture from Coxcatlan, Museo Nacional de Antropología, México, D.F. *(Height: 44 inches.)*

Head of a dead man. Stone sculpture, Museo Nacional de Antropología, México, D.F. *(Height: 14 inches.)*

Alabaster deer found among offerings at the Great Temple of Tenochtitlan. Museo del Templo Mayor, México, D.F. *(Height: 4 inches.)*

Olmec-style jade mask, from Offering 20 at the
Great Temple of Tenochtitlan. Museo del Templo
Mayor, México, D.F. (Height: 4 inches.)

Young woman. Wood sculpture, Museo Nacional de Antropología, México, D.F. *(Height: 14 inches.)*

Obsidian mask. Museo Nacional de Antropología, México, D.F. *(Height: 8 inches.)*

which is the one in red stone that achieves a unique quality; or the case of the fleas, where the artist's observations reached impressive heights. To these are added spiders, centipedes, scorpions, and other creatures, each with their own symbolism. In another vein, an abundant number of gods are represented. Ehecatl, lord of the wind; Xilonen, deity of corn; Xiuhtecuhtli, deity of fire; Mictlan-tecuhtli, lord of the underworld of the dead and the *cihuateteo,* women who died in childbirth, are other examples of their achievements in sculpture. The figure of the commoner, the macehual, also took shape, along with the expression of the face of the warrior and of one who has died, all worked in volcanic stone. To this must be added the minor sculpture in which masks, serpents, and other figures were carved in different types of stone, such as alabaster, jadeite, and obsidian.

The case of painting is different, in that we have only a few surviving examples. The majority come from the excavations at the Great Temple. There we have the painted pillars from stage II, in the temple of Tlaloc, corresponding to the year 1390. On their exterior the pillars have circles reminiscent of the god Tlaloc's eyes. Under them is a blue band with black decoration, and under that, two red bands. Starting there are some alternating white and black vertical lines, which probably represent rain. On the rear of the pillar, which faces the inside of the room, we see a full human figure with skin painted yellow, and decorations — bracelets and anklets — in blue and black. The figure is in profile and seems to have a kind of lance or staff in his hand. He is walking over a current of water. Generally reminiscent of codex figures, these images are the oldest found in the Great Temple.

Other paintings have been found near the main Aztec temple. Examples are the so-called red temples on the north and south, located on both sides of the Great Temple and with an east-facing facade. Both are totally painted, predominantly red

with some designs in ocher, blue, white, and black. One of the painted elements is the knot with two hanging fringes, which we have interpreted as a symbol of the god Huitzilopochtli. There are also some sort of half-eyes or circles that remind us of those eyes associated with currents of water, common in Tenochtitlan. One should not forget that these shrines, in some way, are reproducing elements of the more ancient city Teotihuacan both in their form and in the other materials associated with them. This is the case of the god Huehueteotl, found near the red shrine on the north side, which is a reproduction of a sculpture within the Aztec tradition that clearly imitates the depictions of the same gods in Teotihuacan a thousand years before. We do not doubt, further, that this sculpture of Huehueteotl was located on top of the red shrine.

In the precinct of the eagle warriors, paintings have also been found. In some cases we see true miniatures depicting personages who also remind us of certain codex representations. From the back part of the Great Temple we have figures of skulls and crossed bones in gray and black tones.

To the north of the Great Temple a shrine was found in 1964, on the south wall of which, on an incline, were painted masks of the god Tlaloc. The figures had three white teeth with the characteristic mustache of the god. The coloring was magnificent — blue, orange, white, black — everything contributed to form an abstract idea of the god of water. Thus, in painting we see the same thing as in sculpture. In the same period the Aztecs were creating works that range from an astounding realism to a magnificent abstraction.

In the excavations of the 1960s in Tlatelolco, the other Aztec city, various murals were recovered, but unfortunately they have yet to be studied.

More recently, in 1989, the excavations that we made in Tlatelolco's calendrical temple resulted in the discovery of a very important mural painting. It shows two old characters, a man and a

The Eagle Warriors Precinct near the Great Temple of Tenochtitlan. Museo del Templo Mayor, México, D.F.

Inside of the Eagle Warriors Precinct, near the Great Temple of Tenochtitlan. The relief depicts a flower with four petals that represent the four cardinal directions of the universe. Museo del Templo Mayor, México, D.F.

woman, who by their characteristics remind us of the depiction of the primordial pair Cipactonal and Oxomoco that we see in the *Codex Borbonicus*. In the upper part there are various glyphs of the days that complete the periods of thirteen represented in sculptures around the building. The discovery is important for a better understanding of the religious significance of the building itself as well as for various ceremonial patterns.

Mural paintings were also found in the Aztec ceremonial center of Malinalco. Located about eighty kilometers from Tenochtitlan, its unique

architecture includes temples carved into the rock of a small mountain. In one of them there were remains of a painting showing a procession of warriors, which is not surprising because we know that Malinalco was the site of rituals related to jaguars and to the training of eagle warriors.

Ceramic has been a traditional material in Mesoamerica. The Aztecs managed to give life to clay in bowls, pots, depictions of gods, and so on, and also achieved a high level of control of this material. Such is the case of the two eagle knights discovered in the Eagle Temple just to the north

Tlaloc, the rain god. Polychromed ceramic vessel from Offering 21 of the Great Temple of Tenochtitlan. Museo del Templo Mayor, México, D.F. *(Height: 14 inches.)*

Drawing of the mural found at the calendrical temple at Tlatelolco, depicting Oxomoco and Cipactonal. Museo del Templo Mayor, México, D.F.

of the Great Temple. These magnificent, life-sized figures were formed in four interlocking sections because of their enormous size. The head, the chest and arms, the abdomen and the thighs, and finally the legs were fitted together to make up these impressive ceramic warriors. The face of the individual inside the bird's head, with its enormous beak, is a brilliant example of Aztec aesthetics. The total expression of these figures is not only an example of the extent of utilization of clay the Aztecs achieved, but it succeeds in repro-

ducing the dignity and fierce quality of the warriors of Huitzilopochtli.

We have very little evidence of the dances and music of the Aztecs. Only a few chroniclers' descriptions of certain ceremonies tell us something about this vitally important subject. The *Codex Borbonicus* shows us painted scenes of certain monthly ceremonies, with complicated adornments that imitated specific gods. But the rhythm and other details escape us and are lost to us in time. Nevertheless, the poetry has come to us because after the conquest it could be written in Nahuatl using Spanish characters. Aztec poetry expressed a range of ideas and metaphors found in warrior chants, dedications to the gods, and lyrics reflecting an infinite anguish in the face of death. Here are some examples:[11]

Emeralds,
turquoise,
are your clay and your feather,
Oh, for whom all lives!

Now the princes
feel happy,
with a ritual death by obsidian blade,
with death in war.

Oxomoco and Cipactonal, creator deities, from the *Codex Borbonicus (Academische Druck und Verlagsanstalt, Graz, Austria, 1974 facsimile edition.)*

The rock-cut temple at the ceremonial site of Malinalco.

Terra-cotta figure. Museo Nacional de Antropología, México, D.F. *(Height: 46 inches.)*

Detail of terra-cotta figure. Museo Nacional de Antropología, México, D.F.

Eagle Warrior. Terra-cotta sculpture, Museo del Templo Mayor, México, D.F. *(Height: 75 inches.)*

Huehuetl. Carved wooden drum depicting an eagle, Museo Nacional de Antropología, México, D.F. *(Height: 38 inches.)*

Warrior Zeal

Where the small bells ring the dust rises:
the god is pleased, Giver of Life.

The flowers of the shield open in their crowns,
terror is in the air, the earth shudders.

Here the flowers are acquired, here
in the middle of the plain.

At the edge of war is the beginning, here
in the middle of the plain.
The dust rises, making swirls, with flowers of death.

Don't be afraid, my heart:
There in the middle of plain, I want death by
obsidian blade, our hearts want only death in war.
So there close to war
I am wishing death by obsidian blade.
This is what my heart wants, death of obsidian.

The clouds rise,
the maker of life appears as Spring,
so there the Eagle and Jaguar rub,
there the blossoms open like the fire of the chiefs.

Still, let us be happy,
still, be happy, oh princes,
who in the middle of the plain come to live,
and there we will borrow flowers as a shield,
heat of battle.

Only a Short Time

We torment ourselves,
our house of men is not here . . .
there where the incorporeal are,
there in their house . . .

Only a short time
and earth must be put between here and there!

We live in a borrowed land
here, we, man . . .
There where the incorporeal are,
there in their house . . .

Only a short time
and earth must be put between here and there!

The Anguish of Death

I feel inebriated, I cry, I suffer,
when I know. I say and remember:
    May I never die!
    May I never perish!

What place has no death?
Where is the victory?
    There's where I would go . . .
    May I never die!
    May I never perish![11]

Thus the Aztec managed through various forms of artistic expression to leave us a vision of the world. This vision is peopled by the presence of the warrior and the commoner anguished in the face of death. In this art is expressed the worship of gods and the song of life . . . and of death. It is myth made stone and the reality of those who manage, with great creative power, to converse with their own heart.

A VISION OF TENOCHTITLAN

For an approximate idea of what Tenochtitlan and its neighbor, Tlatelolco, were like, we must begin with their inhabitants. Several attempts have been made to determine how many people lived in Tenochtitlan. Some have exaggerated and spoken of millions. Actually, taking into consideration the population calculated for Teotihuacan and knowing the population of various other cities, it has been calculated that there may have been 250,000 inhabitants in the Aztec capital. Recall that these citizens of Tenochtitlan were socially stratified. The nobles, or pillis, enjoyed privileges that were forbidden to the macehualtin, or common people, who constituted the majority of the population and who were grouped in, or belonged to, different calpullis, or clans, that made up the city. In them were potters, weavers, fishermen, goldsmiths, builders — in short, a complex network of specialists and the important substratum

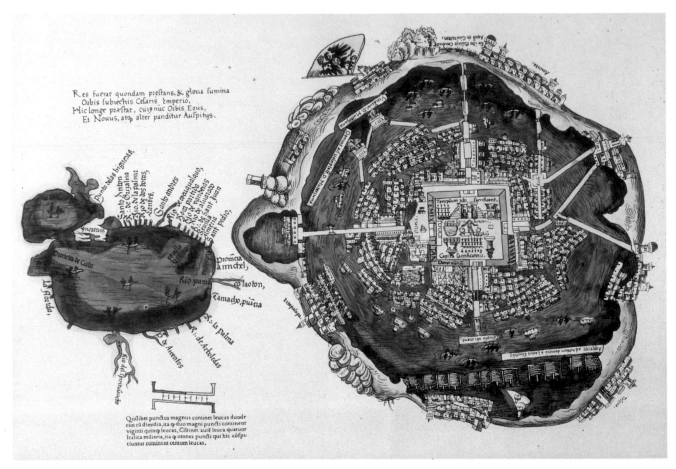

Map of Tenochtitlan, an engraving based on information from Cortés, from the first edition of his letters, *Praeclara Ferdinandi Cortesii de Nova Maris Oceani Hispania Narratio,* published in Nuremberg, 1524.

of the farm workers. As pointed out earlier, the nobles enjoyed many privileges that the common people did not. Remember that they paid no taxes to the tlatoani, which the macehuales did have to do, paying both in kind as well as in contributed labor on public projects such as roads, bridges, and buildings. Nobles occupied public positions; they had their own school; they could have more than one wife; they used certain insignia; and, more important, only the nobility could own land and they were not obligated to work it.

The city was arranged according to a specific pattern. Starting in the center, formed by the ceremonial precinct of Tenochtitlan with its seventy-eight buildings, mostly temples, we see the great causeways running toward the cardinal directions. These causeways were made of firm beds and wooden bridges. The north causeway ran next to Tlatelolco and went to Tepeyac. The west causeway connected the city with Tacuba and Tlacopan. The Iztapalapa causeway ran south to towns such as Mexicalcingo, Iztapalapa, and through connecting branches to Coyoacan, Xochimilco, and Tlahuac. This last group of towns formed part of the chinampa region, where agricultural production, as has been noted, was developed to permit a high output of various plants such as corn, beans, squash, tomatos, chile peppers, and other produce.

Just outside of the aforementioned ceremonial precinct were located the palaces of the great

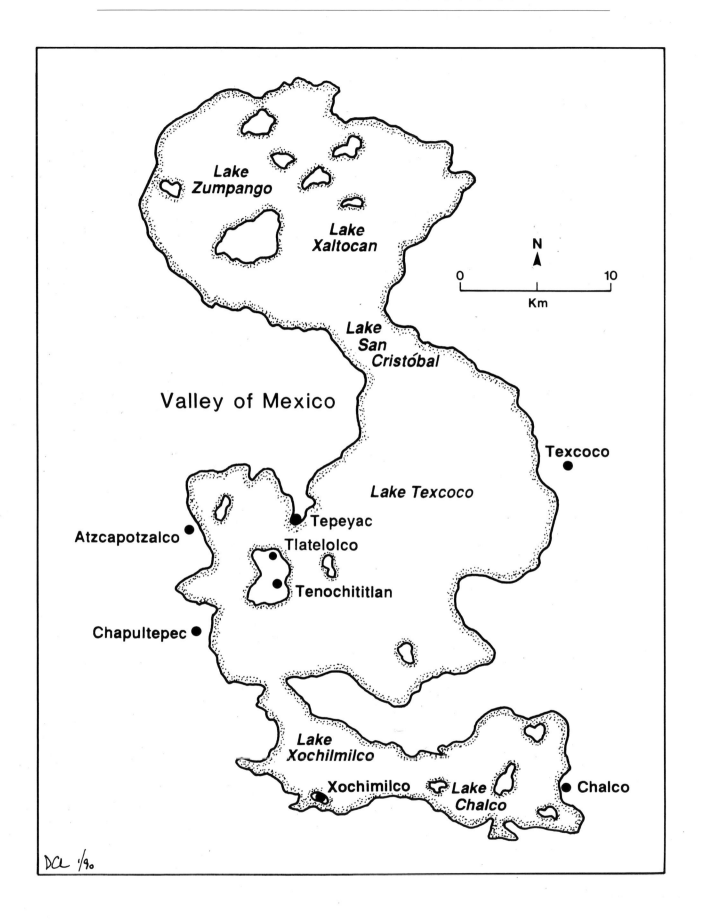

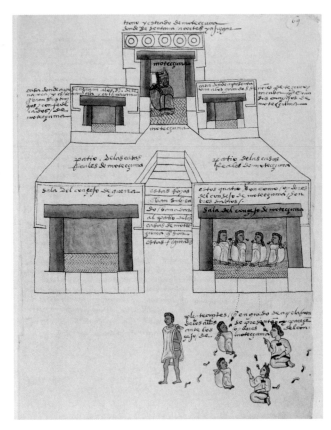

Moctezuma and his palace, from page 69 of the *Codex Mendoza*.

and the city. The shoreline cities had docks to handle the constant traffic of boats. There was periodic flooding, which obliged the inhabitants to take precautions and constantly raise the level of their buildings. The problem of potable water was solved with an aqueduct (built in the epoch of the government of Itzcoatl, 1427–1440), which came from the springs of Chapultepec and which crossed the lake to the city.

The principal market was in Tlatelolco, where one could obtain a great number of products of both local and distant origin. The great quantity and variety of products were impressive. On one side were the pottery stores offering the local production with its typically orange-with-black-stripes motif, or the pottery from Texcoco and even more distant sites. Beyond that were those stands that sold medicinal herbs and other edible plants; farther on, fruits and the various types of birds that were hunted on the lake itself. One could also obtain other aquatic products such as shrimp, fish, frogs, and snakes. There was no lack of textiles made from cotton and feather decorations brought from warmer climes. In short, one could find here every necessity, and everything was exchanged for cacao beans that served as money. The market functioned with its own laws enforced by the pochtecas, or tradesmen, the majority of whom lived in Tlatelolco. This twin city and neighbor of Tenochtitlan achieved significant commercial power and was subjugated by the latter in 1473 during the government of Axayacatl (1469–1481).

lords. The palace of the ruler Axayacatl (located across from the west side of the National Cathedral) is quite well known. The Spaniards were lodged there during their occupation of the Aztec city. The new houses of Moctezuma were found underneath what is today the National Palace. All this indicates that the surroundings of the precinct contained the dwellings of the nobility. Farther from the main ceremonial center, the supreme or sacred space, were the calpullis with their local temples and the houses of their traditional nobility, and the simple houses of the macehuales.

The lakeside character of the city results in a peculiar physical appearance. Let us imagine that next to streets made of dirt or covered with stucco there ran canals of water in which canoes transported people and merchandise. There must have been thousands of canoes that traversed the lake

The many important religious days put in motion a great part of the population. The great public squares were filled with noise, color, exchange, and symbols, for we know that in the pre-Columbian world the people participated in these festivals without entering the temples. That space was reserved for the priests. In the festival of the month of Panquetzaliztli in honor of Huitzilopochtli, for example, a ritual journey involving

Temple Stone dedicated to sacred warfare, found at Moctezuma's palace. Museo Nacional de Antropología, México, D.F. *(Height: 48 inches.)*

Detail of the Temple Stone. At the top, Huitzilopochtli and Tezcatlipoca flank the Aztec solar disk and calendar. Museo Nacional de Antropología, México, D.F.

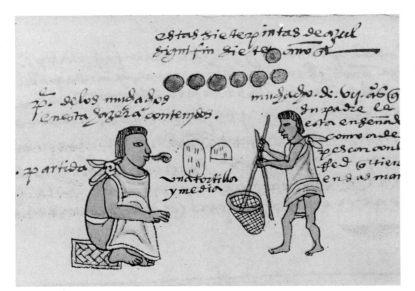

A seven-year-old boy learns from his father how to use a fishing net, page 59 of the *Codex Mendoza*.

A thirteen-year-old boy carries reeds on his back and travels by canoe, page 60 of the *Codex Mendoza*.

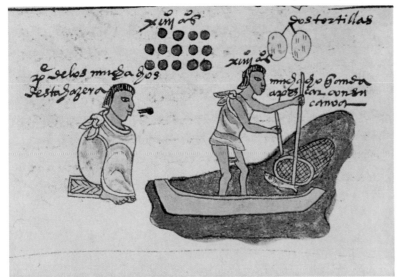

A fourteen-year-old boy fishes from his canoe, page 60 of the *Codex Mendoza*.

The Acuecuexatl Stone. This rectangular stone sculpted relief commemorates the completion of an aqueduct from Coyoacan to Tenochtitlan. Ahuitzotl, the eighth Aztec tlatoani, is shown in the center flanked by a large feathered serpent to the right, and the year sign 7 Reed (1499), the date that the aqueduct was completed, to the left. Museo Nacional de Antropología, México, D.F. *(Height: 12 inches; length: 65 inches.)*

Following page: "The Great City of Tenochtitlan," mural painted
in 1945 by Diego Rivera at the Palacio Nacional, México, D.F.
Moctezuma and the great marketplace of Tlatelolco are depicted
in the foreground.

Two five-year-old boys carry firewood and straw to make brooms, page 58 of the *Codex Mendoza*.

public processions and races was made through various parts of Tenochtitlan and other nearby towns, which created a united sense of purpose. During the festival, they sacrificed the captives that had fallen prisoner in the latest conquests of the tlatoani on the heights of the Great Temple. Thus was repeated one of the great Mexica myths; the re-actualizing of that event in which their god of war had defeated Coyolxauhqui, who commanded the enemy group. This ritual celebrated the triumph of Huitzilopochtli over his opponents.

Speaking of the Great Temple, each time a new tlatoani began to govern, his first official act was to enlarge the temple. This motivated a large number of people to bring the construction materials from nearby areas. Hence, wood, stone, earth, lime, in short, everything necessary for construction, was levied as a tax on the tributary peoples. Also, when rulers wished to carry out works of a public character, the calpulli provided the groups of workers and their foremen. It must have been truly impressive to see the development

A mother teaches her six-year-old daughter to spin thread, page 58 of the *Codex Mendoza*.

A mother punishes her nine-year-old son with a maguey spine, page 59 of the *Codex Mendoza*.

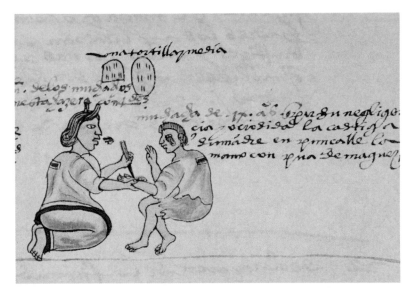

A fourteen-year-old girl learns the art of weaving, page 60 of the *Codex Mendoza*.

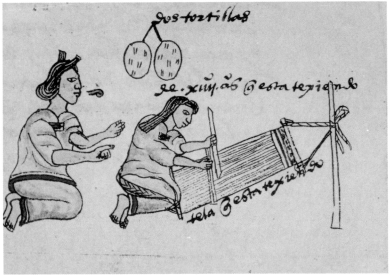

A young man carries branches or boughs used for temple decoration, page 62 of the *Codex Mendoza*.

A man of seventy years enjoys his right to drink liquor, reserved for the oldest Aztec citizens, while a woman merrymaker stands next to a container of pulque, page 71 of the *Codex Mendoza*.

of these communal works that the state required in order to improve the city.

Another relevant event was the moment of departure for war and the return from it. The warrior contingents were composed of members of the calpulli who prepared themselves in the tepochcalli, or schools of the macehuales, in diverse duties, among which was to be warriors. During times of peace each person was devoted to daily activities and care of the cultivated fields. At times of combat these workers were transformed into warriors in the service of their god Huitzilopochtli. We have ventured the hypothesis that in the months dedicated to agriculture, that is, the rainy season, the members of the calpulli were dedicated to the cultivation and care of the planted fields. Once the grain was harvested and the dry season arrived, they were ready for war.

This coincided with their annual calendar, divided exactly into rainy months that were governed by the gods related to water and fertility, such as Tlaloc, Xilonen, the Tlaloque; and the dry months, related to gods of war. The moment of separation between the two parts of the calendar corresponds to the old god of fire, Xiuhtecuhtli. This god is located in the center of the universe and also of the calendar. The symbolic expression of this duality is crystallized in the Great Temple, dedicated to Tlaloc and Huitzilopochtli, that is, to agriculture and war, to life and death.

Moctezuma's Mexico, in which the terrestrial and the symbolic, the above and the below, are united, comes suddenly to its destruction. From the coast arrives alarming news. The Maya have received in a hostile manner those who came in

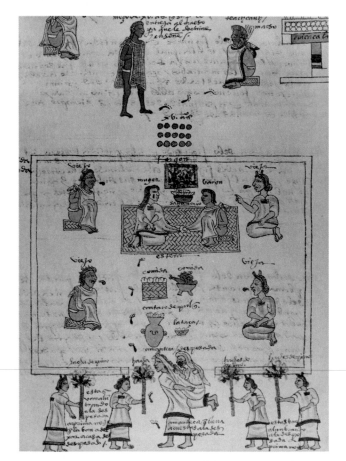

Aztec marriage scene, page 61 of the *Codex Mendoza*.

great ships. But not so the Totonacs, who help the new arrivals, bearded white men, and complain to them of being subjected to the Aztecs in Tenochtitlan.

Moctezuma awaits, impatient, the arrival of the men clad in iron.

AND THE SPANIARDS ARRIVED

We are told by some chronicles that under the government of Moctezuma II (A.D. 1502–1520) several events happened that were taken as omens of the destruction of the Aztec empire. The first warning of what was to happen were the words of the Lord of Texcoco, Nezahualpilli, who was known as a seer and who visited Moctezuma in order to tell him the following:

> Powerful and great Lord: I would greatly prefer not to disturb your powerful spirit, now calm and in repose; but I am forced by the obligation I have to serve you to make you aware of a strange and marvelous thing. . . that is to happen in your time. . . . A very few years from now our cities will be destroyed and devastated, we and our children will die and our subjects will be eclipsed and destroyed.

It is easy to imagine Moctezuma's anxiety on hearing those words. Nezahualpilli continued: ". . . In a few days you will see in the heavens signs that will be an omen of what I say to you." Only a short time later a comet appeared in the sky and could be seen for several days. This greatly afflicted the emperor, for it was taken as the prediction the Lord of Texcoco had made. From that time on, various events began to occur that were seen as ill-fated omens. Moctezuma had ordered a large stone brought to make a *temalacatl,* or gladiator stone, but it never arrived at its destination because it fell into one of the city's canals. The emperor's obsession was such that he ordered the elders to tell him their dreams in order to see if through them he could discover more about the end of the

empire. In one of these dreams the temple of Huitzilopochtli was seen in flames, and the god was overturned and destroyed.

It is known that one of the first notices of the Spanish ships was given to Moctezuma in June of 1518. It must have been the ship of Juan de Grijalva, who arrived at the area of Veracruz that year. Durán's narration describes it thusly: "We saw something in the water, out of which came some white men, white of face and hands and with very long, heavy beards and their clothing is of diverse colors . . . and on their heads they wore round covers." [12]

A year later Hernán Cortés would arrive at the coast of the island of Cozumel and the mainland, only to be received in a belligerent manner by the Maya. Here something very important happens. The Spaniards discover that there are two of their own who had been shipwrecked some time before and who now live among the Indians. Cortés immediately sends for them. They are both Spaniards but quite distinct from each other. They are Gonzalo Guerrero and Jerónimo de Aguilar. The former refuses to join Cortés and points out that he is married with children; that his face is scarified in Maya fashion; that he is a Maya captain in time of war; and that he is totally integrated into the Maya world. To Gonzalo Guerrero and his Indian wife is born the first mestizo. He apparently dies fighting the Spaniards in a later skirmish. On the other hand, Jerónimo de Aguilar is never integrated into native culture. During his captivity with the Maya, he eschews women and reads his Book of Hours. He rejoins the Spaniards and his role is to be fundamental for the conquest of Mexico, for he speaks both the language of the Maya and that of the Spaniards.

Unlike his reception by the Maya, who struggled against him, Cortés's arrival on the coast of Veracruz is not marked by a hostile reception. The Totonacs had been subdued by Moctezuma and traditionally paid him tribute, so the Spaniards represented support for their struggle to throw off the Aztec yoke. Cortés understands this political situation, immediately offers his support the Totonacs, and they form an alliance. The first move is effective. Cortés will take advantage of the peoples subjected by the Aztecs and make them his allies. As Cortés penetrates the central valleys in search of Moctezuma, he knows his indigenous allies will be of great assistance.

Here we should clarify something that at times is misunderstood. Many people wonder how five hundred Spaniards could defeat thousands and thousands of Aztecs. In fact, there were five hundred Spaniards supported by thousands of allied indigenous warriors who had been subjects of the Aztecs and harbored years of anger against Moctezuma's city. To this is added another important factor, the presence of Malinche, that young indigenous woman who was presented to Cortés when the Spaniards reached the coast. She spoke Maya and Nahuatl and could therefore communicate in Maya with Jerónimo de Aguilar, who translated for Cortés. In turn, Malinche translated into Nahuatl, the language of the Aztecs and other peoples of the central plain. With a triangle of languages (Spanish-Maya-Nahuatl), they could understand each other and establish the communication so necessary in these unique circumstances.

The final chapter of Aztec history is short and painful. After numerous vicissitudes and the three-month siege of the cities of Tenochtitlan and Tlatelolco by the Spanish forces and their indigenous allies, the Aztecs are defeated. The last resistance is mounted in Tlatelolco, where on August 13, 1521, the last Aztec emperor, Cuauhtemoc, falls into the hands of Cortés. The emperor is a young man of the nobility, a dauntless warrior who defends his city to the utmost. Exemplar of bravery, Cuauhtemoc does not accept Cortés's repeated demands for surrender. On being taken as a prisoner before the Spanish captain, he speaks these words: "Lord, Malinche, I have done what I am obliged to do in the defense of my city and can do no more, and since I am forced to come as a prisoner before your person and power, take that dagger on your waist and kill me with it now."[13]

These words, which Bernal Díaz del Castillo has left us, spoken in Nahuatl by Cuauhtemoc and translated for Cortés, were not fully understood. What the young tlatoani means is that on being taken prisoner of war he should die sacrificially in accordance with indigenous custom, so that as a warrior he can accompany the sun in its journey, a fate that was provided to those warriors killed in combat and those taken as sacrificial prisoners. He does not ask for a pardon; he asks for the dignified death of a warrior. But Cortés does not understand this and so grants him a "Christian" pardon. The young prisoner wished for death, as his own customs required, more profoundly than the existence he was condemned to live out. Here we have two purposes, two different ways of thinking and being. It is this incomprehension that will determine from that time forward the fate of each of the antagonists: the Indian, subdued and subject to exploitation; the Spaniard, inquisitor and *encomendero,* or feudal master.

Thus culminates the armed struggle and begins the spiritual conquest on the part of the peninsular ideological apparatus represented by the Catholic church. This struggle is equally arduous, as it pits the commitment of the monks on one side and the ingenuity of the Indians on the other as they come face to face in order to impose a new religion or to resist it. All this leads the evangelizing cleric to want to know the history, customs, forms of thought, and social characteristics of the recently conquered society, with the purpose of infiltrating it and casting out what they consider the work of the devil.

In the first years of the colony the task of the missionaries of the first three monastic orders who, starting in 1524, arrived in New Spain — the Franciscans, Dominicans, and Augustinians — is aimed at acquiring a profound knowledge of the conquered groups. The monumental work of Sahagún represents that aim, and so Fray Bernardino tells us in the prologue to his twelve books:

> The physician cannot accurately apply medicine to the sick without first knowing from which humor or from which cause the illness comes; so that it is good for the physician to be learned in his knowledge of medicines and of illnesses in order to apply properly the necessary remedy. Because priests and confessors are physicians of the soul, in order to cure spiritual illnesses it is well that they have experience with spiritual medicines and illnesses. The priest should know of the vices of the republic in order to raise his doctrine against them. For the confessor, in order to ask the necessary questions and to understand what he is told regarding his service, it is well that he know whatever is necessary to perform his services. It is not good that these ministers neglect this conversion, holding that among these people the only sins are drunkenness, theft, and carnality, because there are many other sins among them, and much worse and that greatly need remedy: The sins of idolatry and idolatrous rituals and superstitions and augury and omens and ceremonies have not totally vanished.
>
> In order to preach against these things, and even to know when they exist, it is necessary to know how they were used in their time of idolatry, because if we don't know this they perform idolatrous acts in our presence without our knowing it; and some say, excusing them, that these are foolish or childish acts, because they are unaware that the root from which they come is pure idolatry. The confessors don't ask them about it nor even know that such a thing exists nor do they know their language in order to ask them nor would they understand it if they heard it. Thus, so that the ministers of the Gospel who follow the first who came to this new vineyard of the Lord will have no reason to complain that the first have left in darkness the characteristics of these natives of New Spain, I, Fray Bernardino de Sahagún, professed friar of the Order of Our Seraphic Father Saint Francis, native of the Villa de Sahagún, in Campos, by order of the very Reverend Father, Fray Francisco Toral, provincial of the Provincia del Santo Evangelio, and afterward Bishop of Campeche and Yucatán, wrote twelve books of divine — or more appropriately, idolatrous — and human and natural matters of this New Spain.[14]

The words of the Franciscan show clearly his reasons for writing his books. To this is added the recommendation to the friars to learn the indigenous languages. That results in the proliferation of written vocabularies in the various regions, which will be of use in the evangelizing enterprise. This knowledge of the Indian's customs and beliefs is used to devise different ways of attracting them to the new religion. Some of these practices are well known and can be summarized as follows:

Open atria and chapels: The monks realized that the natives practiced their rituals under the open sky in the large plazas that served this purpose. It was a public worship with collective participation in which the temple itself was only for the priests. The Spaniards responded to this knowledge by making large open-air atria and building open chapels that could be seen by all the participants, since the Catholic rites were traditionally carried out on the inside of the temple.

Collective dances: The monks knew that the indigenous rites were held in the open air and generally involved representations accompanied by collective dances and music. Each festival had its own characteristics. The friars took advantage of this pattern and began to organize true popular theater in which the essential theme was the triumph of Christianity over paganism. In 1538 the *Conquest of Rhodes* was presented in Mexico City, and the *Destruction of Jerusalem* was seen a year later in Tlaxcala. In general, these theater-dances culminated in the generalized baptism of the participating Indians. It is from that practice that we currently see in many towns in Mexico the dances of the Moors and Christians and the Conquest of Mexico.

Prayers in codices: The monks, seeing that ancient writing was based on pictorial codices, began to practice the painting of various prayers to achieve a greater comprehension by the native. Fray Jacobo de Testera excelled in this. Thus, the Credo and the Lord's Prayer were painted and taught by this system.

We could continue enumerating the application of a whole series of practices that had attempted the conversion of the Indian and in which confession also played an important part. All this occured simultaneously, with the destruction of temples, sculptures, and indigenous codices. Fray Toribio de Benavente Motolinía left us a clear description of this destruction, going so far as to compare it with the plagues of Egypt. We will speak of this later, for first we want to include some thoughts on the imposition of Christian images in place of the destroyed idols. It is well worth considering for a moment how the Indian saw the Catholic deities. Let us consider two examples.

From Catholic iconography, several representations will be shown to the conquered in order to try to cast out their gods and create an indigenous interest in the new images. The cross with the crucified Christ is one of them; the other is the figure of the Virgin. Think for a moment about what the Aztecs would see on observing the Christ figure for the first time: a dead individual, bloody — that is, a sacrificed person. The lance wound on the right must have reminded them of the wound made to extract the heart, except that their native priests were more accurate, since they made the wound on the left, where the heart actually is. Christ is placed on a symbol of the old god of fire, for that is what wood formed into a cross is. We should recall that this god (Huehueteotl-Xiuhtecuhtli) ruled in the center of the universe, and from there the form of the cross comes to represent the four directions of the cosmos. This caused not a few clerics to argue that the presence of the cross in these cultures was due to some Christian belief.

Let us now move to the image of the Virgin. We know that Cortés and his troops had images of her, which the imprudent Don Hernán tried to place in the Great Temple until he was dissuaded. But the vital case is that of the Virgin of Guadalupe, who had been worshipped in Spain for centuries. There she played a role similar to that which she would come to have in New Spain. The figure of a dark-skinned Virgin held up by a half-moon served to attract the Muslims, and her name in Arabic is very significant. Her presence in Andalucía provided her an important role in the conversion of those regions. It is possible that her proven effectiveness in Moorish lands was the motive for introducing her in New Spain. And what an effect! Her new apparition in Mexico was to be of great importance, especially when she was located at Tepeyac, a place of pre-Hispanic ritual where a feminine deity was worshipped.

All the foregoing represents the diverse ways employed by the sixteenth-century cleric to impose Catholicism. Nevertheless, as mentioned in the beginning, the native also resisted this imposition. We will give two examples of this resistance.

We refer first to the matter of the destruction of the old temples and the construction of churches, convents, and monasteries. It is the priest Motolinía himself who tells us how the dominated Indian is the one who must build the churches. When the monk who directs the work is not looking, the Indian surreptitiously places sculptures of his gods among the altars and walls of the Christian temple. The Franciscan writes:

> And then equally in Tlaxcala they began to tear down and destroy idols and to put up the image of the crucifix, and they found the image of the crucified Jesus Christ and his blessed mother

The birth of Tezcatlipoca. His left foot is being devoured by the sun as he ascends to the sky. Other symbols around him are characteristic of Tlaltecuhtli, the lord of the earth. Fragment of a stone sculpture once used as a column in a colonial church, Museo Nacional de Antropología, México, D.F. *(Height: 24 inches.)*

Tlaltecuhtli. Detail of circular stone sculpture, Museo Nacional de Antropología, México, D.F.

Tlaltecuhtli, the earth monster. Greenstone sculpture, Museo Nacional de Antropología, México, D.F. *(Height: 34 inches.)*

placed among their idols now that the Christians had given them to them, thinking that they would worship only those; or it was that since they had a hundred gods, they wanted to have a hundred and one. But the friars knew perfectly well the Indians worshipped as usual. Then they saw that they had some images next to their altars along with some demons and idols; and in other places the image was obvious and the idol hidden, or it was behind the altar, and so they took away as many as they could find, telling them that if they wanted to have images of God or of Santa María that they should make them a church. And at first, in order to comply with the friars they began to demand that they give them the images, and to build some sanctuaries and chapels and then churches, and they put images in them, and with all this they always tried to keep their temples safe and sound; although afterward, as things advanced, in order to make the churches they began to make use of their *teocallis* as a source of stone and wood, and in this way they ended up razed and torn down; and the stone idols, infinite in number, not only ended up broken and smashed but they were perfect for the foundation of such a grand and holy work.[15]

The second example is particularly interesting. In the excavations of the Great Temple, and even before, there had been found pre-Columbian sculptures reused and worked into the bases of colonial columns. We see that some represent an effigy of the god Tlaltecuhtli. Why did the Indian choose the images of this god and not any other to convert into the base of the columns? The reason is very clear and we have referred to it earlier in this book. It turns out that Tlaltecuhtli is the lord of the earth, so his figure should be placed on the bottom, that is, out of sight. For that reason the Indian chooses to work the colonial column on top of it, locating his god underneath and achieving its proper location. We can imagine the scene in which the friar walks by the indigenous sculptor and says, "Hey, there is one of your idols

on that stone," and the Indian would answer, "Don't worry, your grace; that part is going face down." The friar walks on while the Indian smiles at having achieved his purpose.

AND THE ARCHAEOLOGISTS ARRIVED

On August 13, 1521, Tlatelolco fell to Hernán Cortés and his indigenous allies. On August 13, 1790, the sculpture of the goddess Coatlicue was found in the main plaza of Mexico City. The Calendar Stone was found shortly afterward. The discovery of these monumental Aztec sculptures had the important consequence of opening the way for the writing of the first archaeological study by Antonio de León y Gama, in addition to political and social repercussions. But it was a simple man who first described the unearthing of the two pieces.

José Gómez was in service in the viceregal palace as a halberdier. (A halberdier is a guard who holds a battle axe as the symbol of his duty.) He crossed the Plaza de Armas (known today as the Zócalo) daily in order to get to the actual seat of political power, and in doing so had to pass in front of the Cathedral, seat of the heavenly powers. The viceroy of New Spain was the second Count of Revillagigedo, Juan Vicente Güemes Pacheco de Padilla Horcasitas y Aguayo, known for his good government in the colony under the mediocre reign of Charles IV in Spain.

José Gómez was a native of Granada, and it is not known for certain what brought him to the colony. What we do know is that he took up the very personal task of writing his *Diary* and his *Notebook,* which, with the passage of time, have come to be documents of great historical value because he recorded in them the notable events of those final years of the colonial epoch. He relates everything that attracts his attention and describes for us in a clear and direct manner, with the

Coatlicue. Detail of the monumental stone sculpture, Museo Nacional de Antropología, México, D.F.

curiosity of a soldier (he reached the rank of corporal) who, with little education, observes and includes situations ranging from religious events to the hangings that were carried out by the justice system of the time.

But what does the halberdier José Gómez have to do with the aforementioned discoveries? It happens that one of the memorable events he reveals to us is, precisely, the discovery and transfer of the sculptures of Coatlicue and the Sunstone, commonly known as the Aztec Calendar Stone. Thus, he says in his *Diary:* "On the fourth of September, 1790, in Mexico, in the main plaza, in front of the royal palace, opening the foundation, they removed a heathen idol, whose figure was a very highly carved stone with a skull on the back

Aztec Calendar Stone (or Sunstone), depicting the four previous cycles of creation and destruction, with Tonatiuh, the Fifth Sun, pictured in the center. Museo Nacional de Antropología, México, D.F. *(Diameter: 141 inches.)*

and on the front another skull with figures of four hands on the rest of the body but without feet or head."[16]

He is describing the sculpture that we know today as Coatlicue, which can be seen in the National Museum of Anthropology. One fact of the discovery is incorrect, however. It was the thirteenth of the previous month that it was found. What may have happened is that the improvements being carried out in the plaza by order of the viceroy, which caused the pieces to be found, were probably not open to the public. For that reason our citizen surely saw the sculpture some days after its discovery and ascribed the find to that date. Don Antonio de León y Gama gives us the correct date in his book *Descripción Histórica y Cronológica de las dos Piedras . . . ,* published in 1792, a book that constitutes the first known study in which the two sculptures are located, interpreted, and sketched. Don Antonio tells us: "Through the legal proceedings it is clear that on the thirteenth of August, 1790, a memorable day because it was the same day on which the city was taken in the name of the king of Spain in 1521 (although two of the witnesses mistakenly say that it was the fourteenth), in the process of excavating the channel for water, the stone statue was found."[17]

We know that the Sunstone was found the seventeenth of December, 1790, as León y Gama set down. José Gómez describes for us how it was moved to the atrium of the Cathedral: "On the second day of July, 1791, in Mexico, they took the stone from the large plaza (which was the calendar of the heathen Indians) to the cemetery of the Cathedral. We don't know where they are going to put it." Later he clarifies this doubt, and we read: "On the third of September, 1793, in Mexico, the stone that served for sacrifice among the heathens was put in the place that they are to put the holy cross, which was in the cemetery of the Cathedral (which faces the Empedradillo)."[18]

Here we need to clarify several things: first, the period in which the Calendar Stone was left in front of the Cathedral (more than two years); and, another point, the character of sacrificial stone that the diary author attributes to it. We do not doubt that by then he had read the *Gaceta de México* wherein these monuments were discussed, or even that he may have read the work of Antonio de León y Gama published in 1792, though that is less likely because it was a very restricted edition sold only by previous subscription.

In reality the work of Viceroy Revillagigedo was enormous in the slightly more than four years that he governed New Spain, especially in matters concerning Mexico City. Gómez records that there never was and never will be a better Viceroy than he . . . and Gómez was right.

The halberdier José Gómez died in Mexico City on the first of February, 1800. He did not live to witness the controversy about those discoveries. He did not know that Coatlicue was buried in the patio of the university near the cathedral because the figure created considerable emotional and ideological uneasiness among the common people who went to see it with lighted candles. He did not know that around 1803 Baron Alexander von Humboldt succeeded in having it disinterred in order to be able to study it, despite the position of the friars who had ordered that it be buried. He did not know that this return to the pre-Hispanic past served in part as a basis for a growing nationalism that ten years later opened the way for an independence movement against Spain.

The discovery of these two archaeological monuments revived attention to the pre-Hispanic world, denied during so many years of colonial control. Perhaps even more important, independent Mexico came to recognize in these discoveries the return to the pre-Hispanic world that had been mutilated and destroyed by the peninsular enterprise. Mexico experienced a collision with its history.

Years and centuries passed after these events. On February 21, 1978, a fortuitous discovery on the corner of Argentina and Guatemala streets, in the heart of Mexico City, would put in motion a research project that would result in the excavation and study of the main temple of the Mexicas, the Great Temple. Five years of work at the site permitted the acquisition of a large quantity of data that enriched our knowledge of Aztec society.

An interdisciplinary team from the Instituto Nacional de Antropología e Historia concerned itself with the analysis of acquired materials. Archaeologists, ethnohistorians, biologists, chemists, and historians, among others, analyzed from their own perspective the remarkable discoveries. The results have been published in more than 150 articles and books, by various specialists, both national and international. The excavations and what they provided stimulated a revitalization of the study of Mexica society. In the words of Dr. Elizabeth Boone, director of Harvard's Dumbarton Oaks:

> In a dramatic reversal the 1978–82 excavation of the Aztec Templo Mayor, coordinated by Eduardo Matos Moctezuma, has . . . given a new impetus to Aztec research. The ritual heart of the Aztec empire, previously known only through description and analogy with other archaeological remains, has been revealed for the first time, and the attention of the public as well as the scholarly community has been turned once again to Aztec studies.[19]

Likewise, Dr. Jacques Soustelle has said that these "extraordinarily interesting excavations, carried out starting toward the end of the decade of the 1970s . . . have brought to light a tremendous amount of new data."[20] And Dr. Colin Renfrew of Cambridge University and Dr. Jeremy Sabloff of the University of Pittsburgh state: "A fortuitous discovery of 1978, however, has transformed the impact of archaeology on our knowledge of the Aztecs and we have been offered an unprece-dented glimpse of remains at the very center of Tenochtitlan."[21]

However, once the Great Temple of Tenochtitlan was studied, it was necessary to return our attention to the ceremonial city of Tlatelolco, a neighboring city that appeared a few years after the former one. They developed together only to be destroyed at the same time by the Spanish conquistadores and their indigenous allies. From 1987 to the present, funds have been provided by the University of Colorado at Boulder to carry out excavations in the ceremonial precinct of Tlatelolco. The results have been important, and recently there has begun a research program under the sponsorship of the Instituto Nacional de Antropología e Historia with research support from the Mesoamerican Archive of the University of Colorado, directed by the historian of religions Dr. Davíd Carrasco.[22] The program will aid in the continuation of work that will allow us to learn more about the city of Tlatelolco, the last redoubt of the Aztecs against the peninsular forces.

The current City of Mexico retains, jealously, the vestiges of the ancient Aztec cities of Tenochtitlan and Tlatelolco. Only sporadically are we able to penetrate the concrete shell of the contemporary city to behold them. Nevertheless, archaeologists manage to break through time and come to know the contexts of the deposited material. They go in search of lost time . . . and they find it.

TRANSLATED BY RALPH KITE

NOTES

1. Miguel León-Portilla, *Los Antiguos Mexicanos* (México: Fondo Cultural Económica, 1976).

2. Fray Diego Durán, *Historia de las Indias de Nueva España* (México: Editorial Nacional, 1951).

3. Miguel León-Portilla's translation of the Florentine Codex is quoted in Johanna Broda, Davíd Carrasco, and Eduardo Matos Moctezuma, editors, *The Great Temple of Tenochtitlan: Center and Periphery in the Aztec World* (Berkeley: University of California Press, 1987), pp. 49–55.

4. Durán, *Historia*.

5. Ibid.

6. Ibid.

7. Fray Bernardino de Sahagún, *Historia General de las cosas de la Nueva España* (México: Editorial Porrúa, 1956).

8. Pedro Carrasco, "La Economía del México Prehispánico," in *Economía Política e Ideología* (México: Editorial Nueva Imagen, 1978).

9. *Historia de los Mexicanos por sus Pinturas* (México: Ediciones Chávez, 1941).

10. Sahagún, *Historia General.*

11. Angel María Garibay K., *Poesía Nahua* (México: Universidad Nacional Autónoma de México, 1965–68).

12. Durán, *Historia.*

13. Bernal Díaz del Castillo, *Historia Verdadera de la Conquista de la Nueva España* (México: Ediciones Nuevo Mundo, 1943).

14. Sahagún, *Historia General.*

15. Fray Toribio de Benavente Motolinía, *Memoriales* (México: Universidad Nacional Autónoma de México, 1971).

16. *Diario del alabardero José Gómez* (México: Universidad Nacional Autónoma de México, 1987).

17. Antonio de León y Gama, *Descripción Histórica y Cronológica de las dos Piedras* . . . (México: Instituto Nacional de Antropología e Historia, 1990).

18. Gómez, *Diario.*

19. Elizabeth H. Boone, "Templo Mayor Research, 1521–1978," in *The Aztec Templo Mayor* (Washington, D.C.: Dumbarton Oaks, 1987).

20. Jacques Soustelle, presentation given at the Symposium on Sacrifice in Mesoamerica at Dumbarton Oaks, Washington, D.C.

21. Colin Renfrew and Jeremy Sabloff, *The Great Temple of the Aztecs* (London: Thames and Hudson, 1988).

22. See the introduction in Davíd Carrasco's *To Change Place* (Boulder: University Press of Colorado, 1990).

TOWARD THE SPLENDID CITY: KNOWING THE WORLDS OF MOCTEZUMA

Davíd Carrasco

One of the most significant developments in human culture in the last five hundred years was the historical appearance of the "New World" in European consciousness. Consider the claim made by Mircea Eliade over twenty years ago in his book *The Two and the One,* in which three great discoveries of the modern world are discussed.

> The discovery of the unconscious could be put on a level with the maritime discoveries of the Renaissance and the astronomical discoveries that followed the invention of the telescope. For each of these discoveries brought to light worlds whose existence was not even suspected. Each, by shattering the traditional image of the world and revealing the structure of a hitherto unimaginable Universe achieved a sort of "break-through."[1]

One such unimaginable universe, which was "revealed" by the Spanish explorations in the sixteenth century, was the cultural area we refer to today as Mesoamerica. This revelation was initiated with the voyages of Cristóbal Colón and reached a culmination, of sorts, with the fall of the Aztec capital, Tenochtitlan, in 1521. Within three quick decades the European image of the world was radically changed and a previously unimaginable universe, Nueva España, America, and above all, the "New World" was discovered, invaded, and invented. As Tzvetan Todorov notes, the discovery

and conquest of Mesoamerica was the "most astonishing encounter of our history," which "led to the greatest genocide in history" and "heralds our present identity" as citizens of the world and interpreters of culture.[2]

We have the vantage point of a grand eyewitness account of a pivotal episode in this transformation provided by Bernal Díaz del Castillo, a sergeant in Cortés's invading army who describes the Spanish *entrada* into the Aztec capital in 1519 this way.

> During the morning we arrived at a broad causeway and continued our march towards Iztapalapa and when we saw so many cities and villages built in the water and other great towns on dry land and that straight and level causeway going towards Mexico, we were amazed and said that it was like the enchantments they tell of in the legend of Amadis, on account of the great towers and buildings rising from the water, and all built of masonry. And some of the soldiers even asked whether the things that we saw were not a dream.[3]

It was a shock to Europeans and it is still a matter of disbelief to many scholars in the United States that the world encountered, violated, and transformed by the missionaries and conquistadores was organized by *altepetls,* or mountains of water, or *tollans,* or places of reeds, the metaphorical names for ceremonial cities. From Cortés's entrada into Tenochtitlan to the subsequent travel accounts and archaeological work in Aztec, Mixtec, Toltec, and Maya ruins of such magnificent cities as Palenque, Tikal, Tula, Monte Albán, Uxmal, and Chichén Itzá, it has been a troublesome discovery that the "Indians" of the New World had developed societies oriented, to borrow the title of Pablo Neruda's Nobel lecture, "Hacia La Ciudad Esplendida," Toward the Splendid City. Returning to Díaz del Castillo's eyewitness description we read of splendid Aztec palaces:

> How spacious and well built they were, of beautiful stone work and cedar wood, and the wood of other sweet scented trees, with great rooms and courts, wonderful to behold, covered with awnings of cotton cloth. . . . And all was cemented and very splendid with many kinds of stone (monuments) with pictures on them, . . . I say again that I stood looking at it and thought that never in the world would there be discovered other lands such as these, for at that time there was no Peru, nor any thought of it. Of all these wonders that I then beheld today all is overthrown and lost, nothing left standing.[4]

This and other eyewitness accounts show that the Spaniards were astonished by the architectural wonders, agricultural abundance, royal luxuries, ritual violence, social stratification, and spatial organization of the capital. To their great surprise, Mesoamerica was an urban civilization organized by powerful, pervasive religious beliefs and practices.

It is becoming clear that the story of Mesoamerica and especially the Aztec world is a story of cities and symbols of cities. The little footprints crossing and looping the ancient maps suggest that these archaic peoples visited such places as Teotihuacan "Abode of the Gods," Xochicalco "Place of the House of Flowers," Colhuacan, "Place of the An-

cestors," and Teocolhuacan, "Place of the Divine Ancestors." In a sense, ancient Mesoamerican history is the story of people and their symbols moving to and from urban centers.[5]

The most impressive urban world encountered in Mesoamerica by the Europeans was the Aztec world of Moctezuma Xocoyotzin, the ruler who was in power in 1519. Earlier in this book, the renowned archaeologist Eduardo Matos Moctezuma writes of the history and ideology of Aztec society on the eve of the conquest. In this chapter I show how humans at the end of the second millennium of Western history work together through interdisciplinary scholarship to understand the sacred spaces and ceremonial actions of the Aztec empire centered in the capital of Tenochtitlan. In the process of describing how we know what we know about the worlds of Moctezuma, I outline some of the major religious patterns and processes that organized and animated the Aztec empire. My presentation places the Aztec world within the broader social and symbolic history of Mesoamerica and then focuses on kinds of resources available for the study of Moctezuma's world to illustrate how interdisciplinary research, including archaeoastronomy, anthropology, archaeology, art history, linguistics, and history of religions, have interacted to carry us to new problems and understandings of *Cemanahuac* (the Land Surrounded by Water), as the Mexica called their space.

CEREMONIAL CENTERS OF MESOAMERICA

The urban character of this brave new world has been described and analyzed in Friedrich Katz's remarkable *The Ancient American Civilizations,* in which the distinguished Latin American historian illustrated how the formation of urban societies in Mesoamerica was the result of developments that

Ballcourt marker. Stone sculpture depicting the face of an animal, Museo Nacional de Antropología, México, D.F. *(Height: 35 inches.)*

took place over thousands of years. The central transformative event of Mesoamerican history was the rise of permanent ceremonial centers that organized the worlds of pre-Columbian peoples.[6] In order to understand the Aztec world of Moctezuma, which was the end product of a number of historical developments, it is necessary to give some attention to the worlds before Moctezuma. As Eduardo Matos Moctezuma ably shows, symbols and ideological remnants of these ancient worlds found their way into the hallowed grounds of the Great Aztec Temple. What we know about pre-Aztec history is that in every case religious symbols, actions, and ideas animated these worlds and were imprinted on their physiognomies. The ceremonial centers were marked by pyramids, temples, palaces, ballcourts, sweat baths, sculpted and painted stairways, and often grand marketplaces. For reasons still difficult to understand, an old Europocentric approach to the New World has deflected scholarship away from a sustained awareness that the ancient Mesoamerican city-state was

the center of cultural life and that this fact has great significance for the meaning of religion and the history of religions in the Americas.

Mesoamerica was a geographical and cultural area covering the southern two-thirds of mainland Mexico, Guatemala, Belize, El Salvador, and parts of Honduras, Nicaragua, and Costa Rica in which the powerful processes of primary urban generation distinguished it as a cultural entity beginning with the emergence of effective food production during the second millennium B.C. and ending with the Spanish conquest in the sixteenth century A.D. The term *Mesoamerica* denoting a cultural and geographical area was introduced by the German ethnologist Paul Kirchhoff in 1943 when he proposed that a distinctive pattern of cultural traits existed in Mexico and parts of Central America that was indicative of urban civilizations. In Kirchhoff's model Mesoamerica was inhabited by a wide spectrum of social groups with various levels of social integration, but the city-state was the most influential social unit.[7] The actual steps leading to

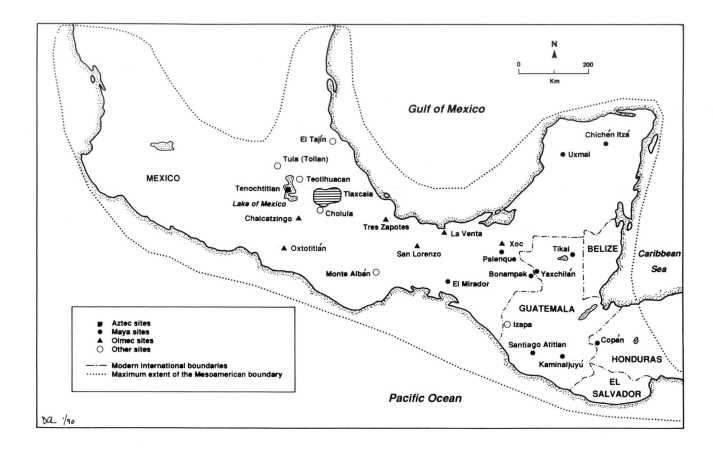

the formation of traditional cities and state societies in Mesoamerica are still only partially understood, but it is clear that the earliest institutions contributing to the integration of societies into urban forms were sacred ceremonial centers. Further, recent research in ceremonial centers in specific and comparative perspective has demonstrated that, while the traditional cities in Mesoamerica functioned as marketplaces, military citadels, and administrative centers, the schedule of social activities had a predominantly religious focus that provided the vital element of sanctified authority for the control of all aspects of society.[8]

Yet it is important to note the striking diversity of urban traditions during the history of Mesoamerican religion. One outstanding characteristic of Mesoamerican history was the eccentric periodicity of settlement and stability. The urban tradition had an erratic pattern marked by political fragmentation, discontinuity in occupation, and decline in the crafts between the successive periods of intensified integrations. This eccentric periodicity was stabilized by such urban-oriented cultures as the Olmec (1200–300 B.C.), Izapan (300 B.C.–A.D. 100), Classic Maya (A.D. 200–900), Teotihuacan (A.D. 200–700), Toltec (A.D. 800–1100), Mixtec (A.D. 1200–1521), and the Aztec (A.D. 1300–1521). This historical pattern is also significant when we realize that Mesoamerica was one of the seven areas of primary urban generation. Egypt, Mesopotamia, the Indus Valley, northern China, Nigeria, and the highlands of Peru as well as Mesoamerica were the places where the profound transformations leading to the creation of the city-state were achieved. In each of these cultures the revolutionary changes that resulted in the original forms of the city were brought into being through the integrative processes of the ceremonial center.[9]

As a means of orienting our journey through

the urbanized worlds of Moctezuma, let us utilize the following description of what the study of the Aztec culture might involve:

> The study of Aztec culture involves the skillful interpretations of *ensembles of texts* (archaeological, pictorial, written, oral, artistic) associated with an array of *ceremonial centers,* in which a nexus of built forms, encoded with cosmological models, historical traditions and hierarchy acted as a *theatre for the performance* of rituals designed to renew the world and enforce the center-periphery dynamics of the urban world.[10]

ENSEMBLES IN THE STUDY OF MOCTEZUMA'S WORLDS

One fascinating problem facing the student of Aztec society and its Mesoamerican background is the abundant archaeological record available for study. As novelist Carlos Fuentes writes about Mexico City, it is a "city witness to all we forget . . . city ancient in light . . . city in the true image of gigantic heaven."[11] As visitors to Mexico know, the presence of the pre-Columbian past is almost everywhere, and many of the ruins and ceremonial centers available for study are not only witness to the Aztec and pre-Aztec past, they were also religious sanctuaries and images of "gigantic heaven." This record of stones and fragments of stones, so abundant in the Aztec case, presents puzzles and problems for the understanding of the Aztec world. One archaeologist, beguiled and frustrated by the problems of studying the archaeological record, has written that "Mesoamerican archaeology has absolutely no coherent and consistent theoretical framework by means of which ritual and religious data can be analyzed."[12] When we turn to the abundant ethnohistorical sources written and collected in Nahuatl, Spanish, French, and Maya languages in the sixteenth century we are also faced with a difficult set of problems, for as the distinguished Mexican anthropologist Alfredo

López Austin notes, "the indigenous sources . . . appear to have been elaborated with malevolent delight in the prospect of confusing future historians."[13]

But we are not the first generation of scholars, novelists, and artists to take an interest in the Aztecs. Benjamin Keen, in his expansive *The Aztec Image in Western Thought,* has shown how the Aztecs have fascinated and at times obsessed Western peoples since the first reports of their existence filtered into Europe in the 1520s. Scholars working with Mesoamerican texts in France, Germany, Great Britain, the United States, and Mexico have generated allied and rival schools of thought on the nature and character of Mesoamerican culture, religion, politics, and art. Major contributions include the works of Eduard Seler, Paul Westheim, and Paul Kirchhoff in Germany, Jacques Soustelle in France, and Alfonso Caso, Wigberto Jiménez Moreno, Pedro Armillas, Miguel León-Portilla in Mexico. Keen shows that such figures as Alexander von Humboldt, Johann Gottfried von Herder, Heinrich Heine, William Carlos Williams, John Drydan, Jean Charlot, Rubén Darío, Napoleon Bonaparte, Hart Crane, Peter Martyr, and Lope de Vega, among many others, were attracted to the cultures and specifically the religious practices of the Aztecs, Mayas, and their neighbors.

This broad response to the Aztecs and their precursors reflects the existence of an abundance of data on religion that is growing yearly as new advances in translation, excavation, and ethnographic research continue. Gaining a holistic or integral picture of the Aztecs is very difficult in part because of the fragmentary nature of the mute and written primary sources, the colonial nature of most of the written works, and the amazing variety of myths, rituals, and ceremonial structures found in these texts. Between us and the pre-Columbian city and its symbols stand not just time and wear, distance and cultural diversity, and renewal with a tradition of wisdom, but also the

Chacmool. Polychromed and stuccoed stone sculpture found on the Tlaloc side of the Great Temple of Tenochtitlan, Museo del Templo Mayor, México, D.F. *(Height: 30 inches; length: 46 inches.)*

conquest of Mexico and Central America and the invention of the American Indian.

Given this hazardous field of diversified and yet abundant evidence, the most useful approach to the problems of texts and context in Meso-america is an "ensemble approach." By ensemble approach I mean a utilization of sources in which the emphasis is on a constant integration of the variety of "texts" rather than aligning oneself with the privilege of a star performance of one type of text. Of course, real advances in our understanding can be made through focusing intensely, for instance on ethnohistorical or literary, linguistic, pictorial, or even archaeological data or combinations of several types of data. But more understanding can be achieved by utilizing a synthetic

or ensemble methodology. The director of the Smithsonian Institution, Robert McC. Adams, stated the point well when he carried out his comparative study of Mesopotamian and Meso-american urban societies based on a "series of structured summaries of syntheses, rather than confining analyses to fragmentary isolated cultural components."[14]

SACRED STONES

Within this commitment to ensembles it is necessary to study the *sacred objects* of Meso-america, as well as the written texts and the oral traditions. In Mesoamerica in general and in the Aztec world in particular some of the most elo-

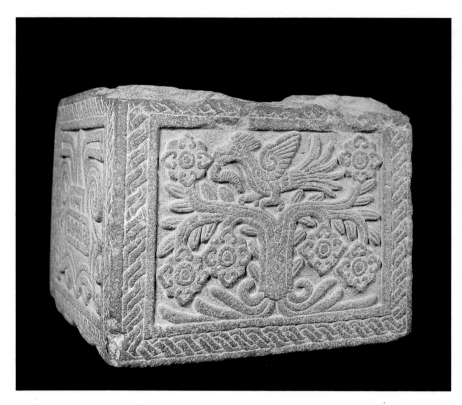

Stone altar dedicated to the astrological cult. An eagle perched in a tree devours a serpent. Museo Nacional de Antropología, México, D.F. *(22 x 28 inches.)*

quent testimony to the power of ceremonial and mythic traditions are the written and painted narratives and images found in "the nexus of built forms," that is, sacred sculptures, monumental temple architecture, pottery, stone masks, and other transformed stones. This material world was imprinted with astronomical events, orientation to the four quarters, sacred histories, narratives of rituals of dynastic successions, warfare, and vision quests.

To see how important the sacred stones and permanent, even monumental ceremonial centers were to the natives, consider how one pre-Aztec pictorial screenfold, the *Codex Vienna* (folios 49a–38c), depicted the primacy of ritual objects and monumental buildings in narrating one of the creative acts of the gods. We see the ancestral culture hero, 9 Wind, ascend into heaven, where he is invested with the implements of kingship by the Creative Pair. He then descends to earth and the earthly world is arranged. When 9 Wind, the ancestor of Mixtec kings, descends down the celes-

tial rope to earth, he is carrying temples and other ritual objects that constitute the first ceremonial center, or city. In this version the ascent and descent of the culture hero (an action typical in many religions) results in the arrival on earth not of written commandments or holy books but the temples and buildings of a ceremonial precinct.

One of the major advances in all of Mesoamerican studies, which illustrates the value of an ensemble approach and the importance of sacred stones, is the excavation of the Great Aztec Temple in Tenochtitlan. This massive penetration into the heart of the Aztec empire has revealed countless treasures and numerous surprises that have had impacts on both our methods and understandings of how the Aztec world was organized and how it influenced the region. Consider this reverie by one of the great interpreters of Aztec philosophy and ethos, Miguel León-Portilla, on the advantages for understanding created by the excavation of the Templo Mayor. "As if it were the realization of a dream, archaeology guides us now in finding,

Circular stone sculpture with solar elements and the calendrical sign 6 Rabbit. Museo Nacional de Antropología, México, D.F. *(Diameter: 18 inches.)*

in the reality of the stones, what remains of the splendid temple with which we were already familiar from description, in the codices, the Nahuatl texts and the eyewitness accounts of the Spanish conquerors."[15]

A prime example of this "dream" discovery can be seen in the 1978 finding of the mammoth Coyolxauhqui Stone by electrical workers digging behind the National Cathedral. For five years truly fabulous discoveries startled public and scholars alike as some seven thousand ritual objects were excavated within the eleven enlargements of the temple situated in the heart of Mexico City. Most of these treasures were obtained from offertory caches including effigies of deities, ritual masks, sacrificial knives, jade beads, marine animals and seashells, human sacrifices, and major and minor sculptures that were deposited together with an enormous amount of animal species. Significantly, a large percentage of these objects came from distant regions of the empire as well as the Pacific Ocean and the Gulf of Mexico. To illustrate our

point about ensembles and sacred stones, let us focus on the discovery and symbolism of the great Coyolxauhqui Stone and the royal myth associated with it.

In the decades immediately following the military conquest of Tenochtitlan, a small number of priests attempted to study the religion and social practices of the Aztecs in order to transform the native culture. The most successful was Bernardino de Sahagún, who worked in three communities in and around the fallen Aztec capital. Among his startling discoveries, which are recorded in a twelve-volume *The Florentine Codex,* was a song, a divine song about the birth of the patron god of the capital, Huitzilopochtli, or Hummingbird on the Left. This fantastic story, reproduced in Chapter 1, told how the Mother of the Gods, Coatlicue, or Lady of the Serpent Skirt, became impregnated by a ball of down that descended into the temple where she was ritually sweeping. When her four hundred children learned of this pregnancy at the shrine they dressed themselves as warriors and

Teotihuacan-style mask, from Offering 20 of the Great Temple of Tenochtitlan. Museo del Templo Mayor, México, D.F. *(Height: 8 inches.)*

The Archbishop's Stone. Monolithic cuauhxicalli found in the house of the archbishop, Calle Moneda, México, D.F. Museo Nacional de Antropología, México, D.F. *(Diameter: 62 inches; height: 26 inches.)*

The Great Tzompantli, stone skull rack from the Great Temple of Tenochtitlan. Museo del Templo Mayor, México, D.F.

prepared to attack the mother at the sacred mountain. The sibling warriors were led by Coyolxauhqui who had incited them into a frenzy and led them on the march to Serpent Mountain. But just before they arrived at the top, Coatlicue gave birth to a fully grown warrior, Huitzilopochtli, who rushed his sister and with his serpent of fire decapitated her in one swipe. The song Sahagún collected goes: "Her body went falling below and it went crashing to pieces in various places, her arms, her legs, her body kept falling."[16] After he defeats the female warrior, Huitzilopochtli turns his might against the other siblings and in a ferocious display of power overwhelms them. He kills many warriors and takes their colors, insignia, and symbols into his own collection. The song ends with the claim that the Aztecs worshipped Huitzilopochtli and emulated him in war.

As is the case with all mythology there are several layers of meaning to this influential story.

At one level Huitzilopochtli's birth and victorious battle against the four hundred siblings represents the solar dimension of Aztec religion. It replays the daily sunrise above the sacred mountain (earth) and the elimination of the moon (Coyolxauhqui) and the stars (centzon huitznahua). At another level this daily experience of nature is viewed in terms of a social conflict, war, and sacrifice. The natural order is a violent order, an order of attack and destruction that provides a warrior theology for the Aztec state.

You can imagine the astonishment of archaeologists and scholars familiar with Sahagún's account when they first gazed on the Coyolxauhqui Stone discovered in February of 1978 next to the National Cathedral. For here was the actual ritual object carved by the Aztecs to tell of the warrior sister's fate. The stone, eleven feet across, depicts in bold relief the dismembered body of the goddess decorated with serpents, a skull, feathers, sandals,

Itzpapalotl, the obsidian butterfly, the descending goddess of war and the earth. Stone sculpture, Museo Nacional de Antropología, México, D.F. *(Height: 30 inches.)*

Profile of Cihuacoatl, the woman serpent. Stone sculpture, Museo Nacional de Antropología, México, D.F.

Teotihuacan-style mask and earplugs, found in Offering 82 at the Great Temple of Tenochtitlan. Museo del Templo Mayor, México, D.F. *(Height: 8 inches.)*

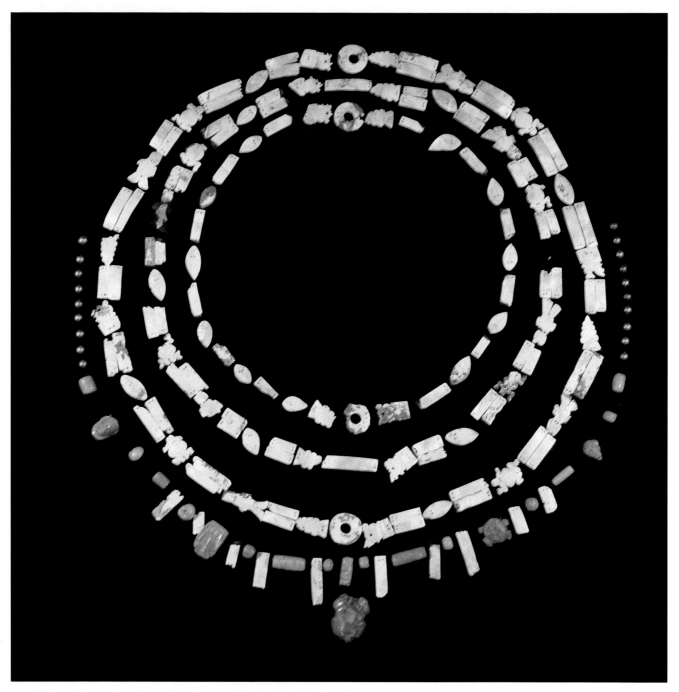

Shell necklace, found in Chamber 3 of the Great Temple of Tenochtitlan. Museo del Templo Mayor, México, D.F.

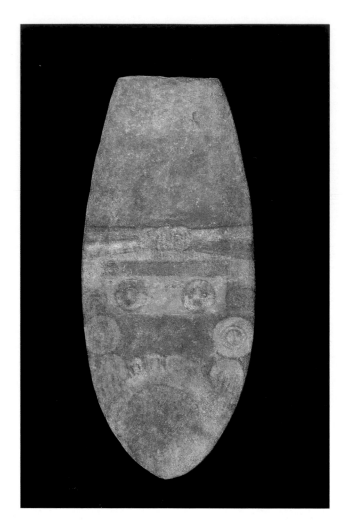

Giant sacrificial knife, polychromed, personified, and depicted in stone. Museo del Templo Mayor, México, D.F.

Giant sacrificial knife, polychromed, personified, and depicted in stone. Museo del Templo Mayor, México, D.F.

Personified flint knives, found among offerings at the Great Temple of Tenochtitlan. Museo del Templo Mayor, México, D.F.

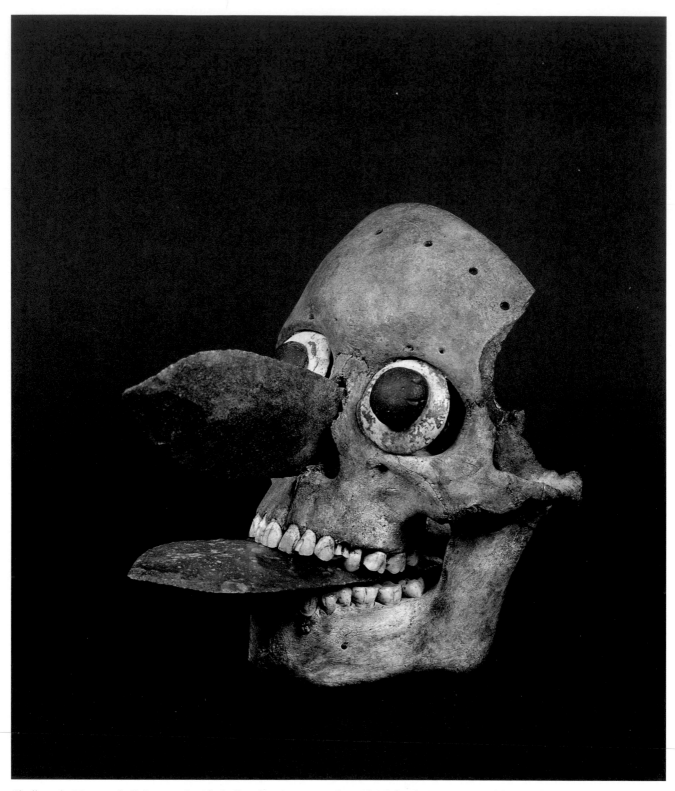

Skull mask. Human skull decorated with shell and pyrite eyes and sacrificial flint knives, Museo del Templo Mayor, México, D.F.

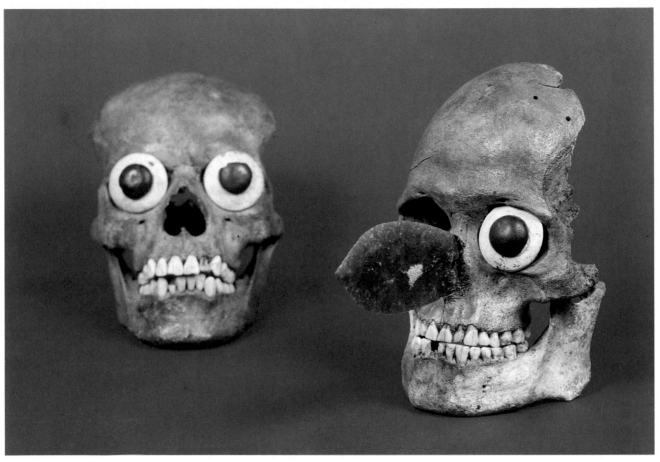

Human skulls, found among offerings at the Great Temple of Tenochtitlan. Museo del Templo Mayor, México, D.F.

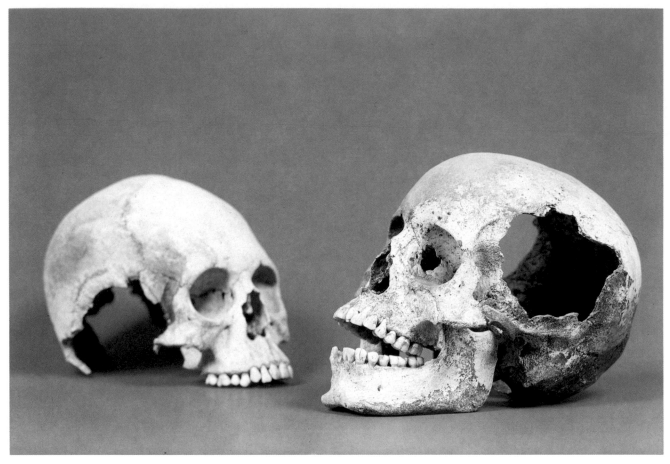

Human skulls, found among offerings at the Great Temple of Tenochtitlan. Museo del Templo Mayor, México, D.F.

Drum with human effigy. Carved in wood with shell and pyrite inlays, from Tlaxcala. Museo Nacional de Antropología, México, D.F. *(Height: 6 inches; length: 24 inches.)*

Giant marine shell, symbol of fertility and life. Basalt sculpture, Museo del Templo Mayor, México, D.F. *(34 x 29 x 17 inches.)*

Stone relief dedicated to the Tlaltecuhtli, the earth monster and lord of the night, depicted as a descending bat with various nocturnal elements. Museo Nacional de Antropología, México, D.F. *(16 x 24 inches.)*

Jaguar Cuauhxicalli. Stone sculpture, Museo Nacional de Antropología, México, D.F. *(Height: 37 inches; length: 89 inches.)*

Mixtec-style ceramic vessel. Museo Nacional de Antropología, México, D.F. *(Height: 8 inches.)*

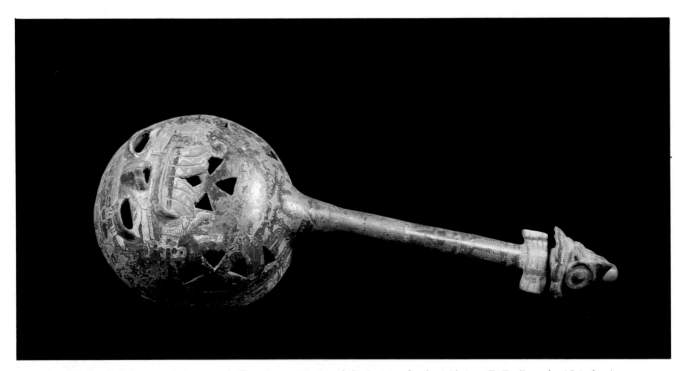

Ceramic Mixtec-syle incense ladle. Museo Nacional de Antropología, México, D.F. *(Length: 18 inches.)*

Polychrome ceramic vessel, Cholula-style, found in Chamber 3 of the Great Temple of Tenochtitlan. Museo del Templo Mayor, México, D.F. *(Height: 13 inches.)*

The Coyolxauhqui Stone. Giant monolith found at the Great Temple of Tenochtitlan. Museo del Templo Mayor, México, D.F. *(Diameter: 128 inches.)*

and precious blood. Equally important, the stone was found at the bottom of the steep stairway leading up to the shrine of Huitzilopochtli, signaling the dominance of the Aztec male warrior over the people of enemy communities. The discovery of this stone clarified what was only previously guessed; that this mythic combat celebrating the victory of Huitzilopochtli was one of the great religious and military paradigms for the world of Moctezuma and his ancestors.

In the case of the Great Aztec Temple we see the efficacy of combining different types of evidence and of giving the archaeological record a prominent place in methods of study.

TWO CONTROVERSIES

Our discussion about ensembles and archaeological sources reflects two of the major controversies that have arisen in recent years about the world of Moctezuma. The first is whether the Aztecs and their predecessors attained a level of social and symbolic complexity associated with urban civilizations. Did ancient peoples in the Americas build cities or some less complex form of society? The second controversy, reflected in the myth and stone just discussed, is whether human sacrifice and cannibalism took place, and on a large scale; and if so, why?

Each of these issues has involved heated and sometimes fantastic formulations. For instance, in his article "Montezuma's Dinner," written in 1876, one of the founders of cultural anthropology, Lewis H. Morgan, claimed that the Aztecs were "still a breech cloth people wearing the rag of barbarism as the unmistakable evidence of their condition." Morgan had developed a scheme of human society's progress through three stages — Savage, Barbarism, Civilized — and argued that the Aztecs and their neighbors had only developed to the stage of Barbarism. Further, the Aztec palaces described by Hernán Cortés and Bernal Díaz del Castillo were, according to Morgan, writing of them 350 years later, "joint tenement houses" that "reflected the weakness of the Indian family and ability to face alone the struggle of life." That the barbarian chief Moctezuma might have eaten on a tablecloth scandalized Morgan, who wrote: "There was neither a political society nor a state, nor any civilization in America, when it was discovered and excluding the Eskimo, but one race of Indians, the Red Race."[17]

While Morgan's thesis was very influential well into the twentieth century, subsequent research by archaeologists and ethnohistorians has shown that it is not a question of whether native Americans developed cities or not, but: what kinds of cities did they develop? The Aztec capital was an imperial city that controlled or struggled to control the tribute, political power, and agricultural abundance of over four hundred other communities in central Mesoamerica.

More recently, in 1979, a furious controversy broke out in academic journals and books concerning what Marvin Harris called the "Cannibal Kingdom" of the Aztecs. At the center of the storm were the extraordinary ritual practices of bloodletting, human sacrifice, and ritual cannibalism practiced by Mesoamerican peoples. The debate, revived by the excavation of the Great Aztec Temple, divided into two camps: the ecological explanation, which stated "they ate humans for protein and profit"; and the cultural explanation — "they were ritually exchanging gifts with the gods in the forms of things, hearts, skulls, and blood." As we shall see, Aztec religion was animated, in part, by ritual bloodletting and the sacrifice of human beings who were ritually transformed into deities. Regardless of which position you take on these controversies, the best results will come by using the ensemble approach to evidence.

Kneeling goddess. Stone sculpture, Museo Nacional de Antropología, México, D.F. *(Height: 44 inches.)*

Rectangular stone relief depicting *zacatapayolli,* the grass ball of human sacrifice, found at Huitzuco. Museo Nacional de Antropología, México, D.F. *(Height: 38 inches.)*

Stone vessel depicting zacatapayolli, the grass ball of human sacrifice. Museo Nacional de Antropología, México, D.F. *(Diameter: 40 inches.)*

Personage with Ehecatl mask. Basalt sculpture, Museo Nacional de Antropología, México, D.F.
(Height: 26 inches.)

Seated person with Ehecatl mask. Basalt sculpture, Museo Nacional de Antropología, México, D.F. *(Height: 20 inches.)*

Personage with the features of Tlaloc, the Aztec god of rain and fertility, holding a small human skull. Stone sculpture, Museo Nacional de Antropología, México, D.F. *(Height: 28 inches.)*

PICTORIAL AND ETHNOHISTORICAL EVIDENCE

In the fall of 1985 a Mexican journalist visiting France was given permission to study the Aztec ritual manuscript, the *Tonalamatl Aubin,* in the confines of the rare books room at the Musée de l'Homme (*Tonalamatl* = book of days). With a certain stealth and unusual luck, he stole the manuscript from the museum, fled to Yucatán, Mexico, and eventually announced in the newspapers that he had returned an indigenous treasure to its homeland. While the two governments disputed the rightful ownership of the *Aubin,* the journalist became something of a national hero.

The cultural pride associated with the recovery of the *Tonalamatl Aubin* symbolizes the rich resources of the surviving pictorial manuscripts for studying the Aztec world and its precursors. It is amazing that eleven of the thousands of pre-Columbian pictorial manuscripts, depicting the genealogies, histories, and cosmologies of indigenous peoples, survived at all. For instance, Hernán Cortés's march from Villa Rica de la Vera Cruz to Tenochtitlan was punctuated with the defacing, whitewashing, and removal of religious monuments and images. In case after case the Spaniards destroyed the images of deities and ceremonial life, replacing them with Christian crosses on the spot. Later, in 1535, the apostolic inquisitor of Mexico, Juan de Zumárraga, ordered the collection and destruction of the pictorial records belonging to the Nahuatl cultural capital of Tezcoco. Tradition tells us that the beautiful painted historical, ritual, and genealogical screenfolds were gathered into a huge pile in the local marketplace, set afire, and turned to ashes. It is a bitter fact that of the hundreds of pictorial manuscripts extant in Mesoamerica in 1517 only eleven remain today.

While most of the surviving manuscripts come from areas outside and prior to the Aztec empire, one of the most outstanding manuscripts, produced very close to the time of conquest, the *Codex Borbonicus,* contains ritual scenes that reveal remarkable patterns of life during the reign of Moctezuma II. Let me focus on one great ceremony of social and cosmic renewal as a means of describing ritual human sacrifice, astronomy, and the response of the common person.

THE NEW FIRE CEREMONY

On a morning in the middle of November in 1507, the fourth year of Moctezuma's reign, a procession of fire priests with a captive warrior "arranged in order and wearing the garb of the gods" processed out of the capital of Tenochtitlan toward the ceremonial center on the Hill of the Star. During the days prior to this auspicious night, the populace of the Aztec world participated together in the ritual extinction of fires, the casting of statues and hearthstones into the water, and the clean sweeping of houses, patios, and walkways. In anticipation of this fearful night, women were closed up in granaries to avoid their transformation into fierce beasts who would eat men, pregnant women would put on masks of maguey leaves, and children were punched and nudged awake to avoid being turned into mice while asleep. For on this one night in the calendar round of 18,980 nights, the Aztec fire priests celebrated, "when the night was divided in half," the New Fire Ceremony that ensured the rebirth of the sun and the movement of the cosmos for another fifty-two years. This rebirth was achieved symbolically through the heart sacrifice of a brave captured warrior specifically chosen by the king. We are told in Sahagún's account that when the procession arrived "in the deep night" at the Hill of the Star the populace climbed onto their roofs, and with unwavering attention and necks craned toward the hill they became filled with dread that the sun would be destroyed forever.

The accompanying illustration from the *Codex*

The New Fire Ceremony, from the *Codex Borbonicus* (Academische Druck und Verlagsanstalt, Graz, Austria, 1974 facsimile edition).

Borbonicus shows the fire priests bringing ritually prepared bundles of wood to the sacred fire where it will be consumed. These bundles represent the previous fifty-two-year time period, and their combustion creates the New Fire and the new cosmic era. This illustration, when joined to Sahagún's informants' descriptions, enhances our sense of Aztec costume, symbolism, and ritual action.

It was thought that if the fire could not be drawn the demons of darkness would descend to eat men. As the ceremony proceeded, the priests watched the sky carefully for the movement of a star group known as Tianquiztli, or Marketplace, the cluster we call the Pleiades. As it passed through the meridian, signaling that the movement of the heavens had not ceased, a small fire was started on the outstretched chest of a warrior. The text reads: "when a little fire fell, then speedily the priests slashed open the breast with flint knife, seized the heart, and thrust it into the fire. In the open chest a new fire was drawn and people could see it from everywhere." The populace cut their ears, even the ears of children in cradles, the text tells us, and "spattered their blood in the ritual flicking of fingers in the direction of fire on the mountain." Then the New Fire was taken down the mountain and carried to the pyramid temple of Huitzilopochtli in the center of the city of Tenochtitlan, where it was placed in the fire holder of the statue of the god. Then, messengers, runners, and fire priests who had come from everywhere took the fire back to the cities, where the common folk, after blistering themselves with the fire, placed it in their homes, and "all were quieted in their hearts." [18]

This dramatic performance, so plainly described in Sahagún and so colorfully depicted in the pictorial manuscript, shows new dimensions of Moctezuma's world to us. The New Fire Ceremony was also called *Toxiuhmolpilia,* or Binding of the Years, and actually tied together two important but very different ceremonial centers: the Great Temple of Tenochtitlan and the Hill of the Star. This rare ceremony, usually seen only once in a lifetime, began in the capital when the ruler Moctezuma ordered a captive warrior be found whose name contained the word *xihuitl,* meaning turquoise, grass, or comet, a symbolic name connoting precious time. The procession of priests and deity impersonators moved along a prescribed passageway, presumably seen and heard by masses of people before arriving at the Hill of the Star. In another report of this ceremony we are told that Moctezuma had a special devotion and reverence for this hill and shrine. Then, having walked the twenty kilometers and climbed the ceremonial hill, the group of priests and lords, sharing a heightened sense of expectation and fear, sought another procession, that is, the procession of the stars through the meridian. Once the procession of stars was recognized, the heart sacrifice was carried out and the new fire was lit amid universal rejoicing and bleeding. Next in the primary action that links the two centers, the fire was taken back to the Templo Mayor in the center of the Aztec capital. Then, in what is the most meaningful social and symbolic action, messengers, priests, and runners who had "come from all directions" to the Templo Mayor took the fire back to the towns and cities of the periphery, where it ignited the New Fire, or time periods, locally. In this way, all the units of the society, with their local shrines, were re-illuminated by the New Fire that linked them to both the capital and the sacred hill. The fiery display ignited the imperial landscape by linking up all the sacred spaces of the Aztec world.

We also see the importance of sacred time in the Aztec world in the New Fire Ceremony. Aztec life was organized by two major calendar rounds, a 365-day solar cycle and a 260-day ritual cycle. Both calendars were divided into months that were marked by carefully choreographed ritual performances and processions involving different cults, priestly groups, and communities. Aztec priests interlocked these two cycles together, noting that all the possible interactive combinations became exhausted after 18,980 days, or every fifty-two years. The end of this great cycle marked a point of cosmological crisis and transition. The New Fire Ceremony, focused on the heart sacrifice of a captive warrior, functioned to renew the beginning of these cycles for another fifty-two years.

SACRED WORDS — THE ORAL LITERATURE

It is erroneous to think of Aztec society and religion as concerned only with violence and aggression. As the pictorial images and ethnographic texts show, Nahuatl-speaking peoples worked cooperatively in farming communities, developed exquisite crafts and art forms, sponsored poetry festivals, cared deeply for children, worried about the power of gossip, loved telling stories, and warmed to the excitement, color, and tensions of the marketplace. As one of the priests wrote after spending twenty years with the Mexicas, "no people love their children as much as these people." All of these activities, the human life cycle, cultural displays, farming, and trading, were regulated and renewed by ceremonial performances.

One of the most refined and influential art

forms was human speech. It is not easy for people raised in a culture where "free speech" is a leading influence in communication to appreciate the power and meaning of those languages based on traditionally formal speech patterns and expressions. Nahuatl was a highly formalized language, which has often led outsiders to misunderstand its intentions and meanings. For instance, when Moctezuma Xocoyotzin greeted Hernán Cortés he used royal Nahuatl polite speech, which elevated the Spanish leader to a level of high honor. A number of scholars unfamiliar with the Aztec language arts wrongly concluded that the welcoming speech showed the ruler to be a weak and docile leader. In fact, he was greeting a state visitor in the proper royal style of a welcoming tlatoani, or chief speaker.

Spanish priests who labored to learn the spoken language of Nahuatl during the early decades after the conquest discovered how florid, elegant, and symbolic the various Indian languages were. One of the finest testaments to the linguistic genius of the Aztecs is *Book VI* of the twelve-volume *Florentine Codex*. Titled *Rhetoric and Moral Philosophy*, it contains forty extensive prayers, some over four pages long, plus orations spoken by parents, rulers, midwives, and citizens. This volume concludes with a collection of proverbs, riddles, and metaphors portraying wit, insight, and religious imagery of Aztec life. As a means of illustrating the character of the spoken language of Moctezuma's world, I will discuss four dimensions of Aztec verbal arts: (1) the *tlamatinime,* or wise men trained in verbal arts; (2) the *huehuetlatolli,* or the Ancient Word; (3) riddles; and (4) poetry of war.

The Tlamatinime

Rhetorical skills were appreciated in many social situations, but the refinement of speech was under the direction of a group of trained specialists, tlamatinime (knowers of things), who used the art of language to raise philosophical questions about human nature and its relationship to ultimate truth. These specialists used language to communicate and make offerings to the gods.

Compared to a "stout torch that does not smoke," the tlamatinime were trained in calmecacs, or schools of higher learning, to be ideal guides in human affairs. They preserved honored tradition, produced and read the painted manuscripts, and developed metaphors and poems to probe the true foundations of human existence. The clearest examples of their verbal art come from a series of texts showing the talents and insights of such rulers as Nezahualcoyotl (Fasting Coyote), king of Tezcoco, Tecayehuatzin, prince of Huejotzinco, and a dozen other tlamatinime. Indications are that this type of verbal art was largely practiced by the elites.

These poet-philosophers saw human existence as essentially fragile and ephemeral, as this poem attributed to Nezahualcoyotl indicates.

> I comprehend the secret, the hidden:
> O my lords!
> Thus we are,
> we are mortal,
> men through and through
> we all will have to go away,
> we all will have to die on earth.
> Like a painting,
> we will be erased.
> Like a flower,
> we will dry up
> here on earth . . .
> Think on this my lords,
> eagles and ocelots,
> though you be of jade,
> though you be of gold
> you also will go there
> to the place of the fleshless.[19]

The precious aspects of life symbolized here by jade, gold, and flowers are seen as transitory and vulnerable rather than solid and with a firm foundation. Faced with this condition of instability and illusion, the tlamatinime developed a verbal strategy aimed at discovering and experiencing the nature of truth, a solid foundation to existence. They believed that there was such a reality beyond human existence, "in the region of the gods above and in the region of the dead below." In order to penetrate these regions and discover a stable reality, they had to devise techniques to open the depths of the human personality to the illusive world of truth. The main technique was the creation of *in xochitl, in cuicatl,* or flowers and birdsongs, meaning artistic expressions in the forms of words, songs, and paintings that connected the human personality with the divine world. Writing of this connection, the Fasting Coyote stated:

My flowers will not come to an end,
my songs will not come to an end,
I, the singer, raise them up:
they are scattered, they are bestowed.[20]

Speaking of the power of poetry to express a lasting truth, he wrote:

Even though flowers on earth
may wither and yellow,
they will be carried there,
to the interior of the house
of the birth with the golden feathers.[21]

This approach of linking the "face and heart" or human personality to the divine world through the medium of "flower and song" was based on a religious conception of duality. As we saw in Eduardo Matos's chapter, Nahuatl culture was based on a supreme Dual God, Ometeotl, who created the cosmos and maintained it. This duality was manifested in the dualities that combined to make forms of reality such as male/female,

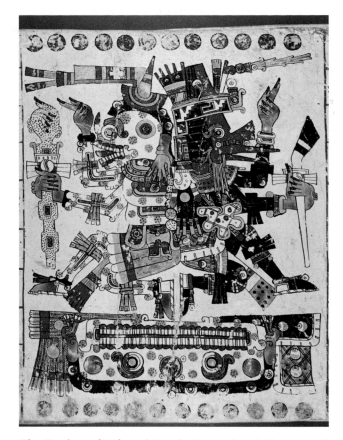

The Duality of Life and Death, Quetzalcoatl Ehecatl and Mictlantecuhtli, from the *Codex Borgia* (Academische Druck und Verlagsanstalt, Graz, Austria, 1976 facsimile edition).

hot/cold, left/right, underworld/celestial world, above/below, darkness/light, rain/drought, death/life. At the level of human language this duality could be expressed in metaphors that generally consisted of two words or phrases joined to form a single idea, like "flower and song" equaling poetry or truth. At the level of the gods, the High God or Ometeotl (Giver of Life) was the combined forces of the male and female creators Ometecuhtli and Omecihuatl. The language form used to inculcate this divine duality into words, called by Mexican linguists a *difrasismo,* includes two phrases joined to mean one thing. Besides in xochitl, in cuicatl, flower and song equals poetry, the truth, we find:

Stone relief depicting a jaguar and an eagle speaking *atl tlachinolli*, the sacred words of warfare, representing the jaguar and eagle warriors. Museo Nacional de Antropología, México, D.F. *(14 x 20 inches.)*

In atl, in tepetl = water and hill = a town

In topan, in mictlan = what is above us, the region of the dead = the world beyond humans

Topco, petlacalco = the skirt, the blouse = the sexual nature of women

Huehuetlatolli

One of the most influential instruments for organizing human behavior was the huehuetlatolli, or the Ancient Word. These rhetorical orations were florid, elegant metaphorical speeches that were memorized and presented at a number of ceremonial occasions such as the coronation of a ruler, the entry of a youth into the calmecac, the work of a midwife, or a marriage ceremony. Consider the beauty and tenderness expressed in this huehuetlatolli spoken by a midwife to a baby who had been born. Note how this formal speech required in midwife training reflects the relations between cosmos and human body as well as divine duality and human language.

And when the baby had arrived on earth, then the midwife shouted: she gave war cries, which meant that the little woman had fought a good battle, had become a brave warrior, had taken a captive, had captured a baby. . . .

If it was female, she said to it: "My beloved maiden, my youngest one, noblewoman, thou has suffered exhaustion, thou hast become fatigued. Thy beloved father, the master of the lord of the near, of the nigh, the creator of men, the maker of men, hath sent thee: . . .

"My youngest one! Perhaps thou wilt live for a little while! Are thou our reward? Art thou our reward? Art thou our merit? Perhaps thou wilt know thy grandfather, thy grandmothers, thy kinsmen, thy lineage.

"In what way have thy mother, thy father Ometecuhtli, Omecihuatl, arrayed thee? In what manner have they endowed thee?"[22]

Riddles

It is evident that the Aztecs loved word play as much as they loved words. While the Nahuatl language arts were florid, noble, and highly formal, they also contained a capacity for word pictures and wit. Riddles were part of the daily speech acts, as the informants of Sahagún made clear. Knowing the correct answer to riddles indicated that a person was from a good family. Note the ways that humans and nature are linked in these riddles as you try to figure out their meaning.

What is a little blue-green jar filled with popcorn? Someone is sure to guess our riddle; it is the sky.

What is a mountainside that has a spring of water in it? Our nose.

What is a warrior's hair-dress that knows the way to the region of the dead? Someone is sure to guess our riddle: it is a jug for drawing water from the well.

What is it that goes along the foothills of the mountain patting out tortillas with its hands? A butterfly.[23]

Poetry of War

It is important to place some of these aesthetic creations within their actual social context. As stated earlier, Aztec society was not solely engulfed in warrior ideology. Nevertheless, the practice and imagination of war permeated the arts of Moctezuma's world. The several hundred surviving Aztec poems, composed in either the fifteenth century preconquest or sixteenth century postconquest society, were produced by Aztec nobles who supported the cause of war and domination in their world. While it is true that some poetic creations reflect a concern with a world beyond sacrifice and warfare, the majority reflect a commitment to the imperialism of the Aztec state.[24] An example of the first type of poetic creation appears in this fragment from the *Cantares Mexicanas:* "Friends, take pleasure! Let us put our arms around each other's shoulders here. We're living in a world of flowers here. No one when he's gone

Jaguar warrior with a captive, page 64 of the *Codex Mendoza.*

can enjoy the flowers, the songs, that lie outspread in this home of the Giver of Life. Earth is but a moment. Is the Place Unknown the same?"[25] Here we see a world where caring, sensitive human relations are sought after and emphasized. However, many poems, previously thought to be only about the themes of artistic wisdom, have shown upon further scrutiny to be veiled or direct references to war, bloodshed, and human sacrifice. In fact, there appears to be a poetic parallelism between the beauty of flowers and the beauty of warfare.

One recent study has shown how the creation of Aztec poetry was closely tied to Aztec imperialism. This poetry was a court and temple art patronized by the Aztec royal lines in various ceremonial cities. Driven to create an understructure of

Detail of the Archbishop's Stone. A warrior takes a captive by the hair in battle. Museo Nacional de Antropología, México, D.F.

A water monster in the image of a dog, symbol of Ahuitzotl. Stone sculpture, Museo Nacional de Antropología, México, D.F. *(16 x 16 inches.)*

Sacrificial stone. Basalt sculpture, Museo Nacional de Antropología, México, D.F. *(Height: 18 inches.)*

ideological support for conquest and domination, these royal houses had poets commemorate battles, heroes, sacrifices, and victories. These poems and their presentations were used as part of the ceremonial theater that displayed captive warriors, involved them in mock battles against the eagle and jaguar warriors of the capital, and finally sacrificed them in vivid displays of political imagery.

In order to ensure a steady stream of poets and poetry (to accompany the sacrifices) the rulers set up *cuicacalli,* or houses of song, where specialists in poetic themes, music, and choreography were employed to provide theater for the great festivals. Once compositions had been completed, poets and dancers would be sent to the various neighborhoods, and a town crier would call the people to a meeting so that the songs could be learned and memorized. This method ensured that children and especially young warriors in training would hear, sing, and dance the religious ideology of the world of Moctezuma.

What seems remarkable is that this poetry presented warfare not primarily as an act of political force but as an artistic act in which warriors, especially warriors who capture enemies, are seen as poets. Consider this poem celebrating the prestige of nobles in war:

> Nobles and kings are sprouting as eagles, ripening as jaguars, in Mexico: Lord Ahuitzotl is singing arrows, singing shields. Giver of Life, let your flowers not be gathered! . . . You've adorned them in blaze flowers, shield flowers.[26]

As flowers sprout in nature so nobles sprout as eagle warriors, and as poets sing songs containing the duality of the gods, the ruler Ahuitzotl sings arrows and shields as he is transformed in battle into a religious force. The Aztec poets turn the battlefield into a garden of religious beauty where "blaze flowers," warriors, avoid the magical transformation of death. The battlefield is where "Jaguar flowers are opening, knife death flowers are becoming delicious upon the field."[27]

THE RETURN OF QUETZALCOATL

One of the great stories that influenced Aztec life as well as the collapse of Moctezuma's world was the story of Quetzalcoatl, the Plumed Serpent. Quetzalcoatl appears in the surviving sources as both a creator god and as an ideal priest-king. Perhaps there were three different but intertwined Quetzalcoatls: (1) the Feathered Serpent God of many peoples in Mesoamerica; (2) the Toltec priest-ruler of Tollan; and (3) the Quetzalcoatl who was identified with Cortés during the early days of Spanish and Aztec encounters. In what follows I discuss all three as a means of illustrating both the pre-Hispanic tradition of Quetzalcoatl and the puzzle of his identification with the Spaniards in 1519.

One passage, recited by Aztec elders to the Spanish priest-researcher Bernardino de Sahagún, goes:

> Quetzalcoatl was looked upon as a god. He was worshipped and prayed to in former times in Tollan, and there his temple stood: very high, very tall. Extremely tall, extremely high.[28]

This passage refers to the powerful creator god Quetzalcoatl, who had many roles in the cosmic formation of the Mesoamerican world. He was one of the four children of the divine duality, Ometeotl, who dwelled in the innermost part of heaven, above the twelfth level. In different types of sources surviving the conquest, we find that this god Quetzalcoatl was renowned for liberating corn buried deep in Sustenance Mountain for human use, and in another guise dove into Mictlan, the underworld, in order to retrieve the bones of ancestors, and in other accounts participated in the celestial conflicts that drove the cosmos through several of its creations and destructions. It is clear that Quetzalcoatl was revered in many parts and periods of Mesoamerican history and often associated with the major temple precincts that gave communities a sense of orientation and purpose.

The ethnohistorical record also shows the creative powers of another Quetzalcoatl, a human ruler (or it may be there were several such leaders) who was the living image on earth of Quetzalcoatl's power and authority. The most outstanding example of this *hombre-dios* (man-god) Quetzalcoatl was called Topiltzin Quetzalcoatl (Our Young Prince the Plumed Serpent), who ruled in the "Great Tollan" sometime around the tenth century. The Great Tollan was a city-state consisting of over twenty sizable settlements surrounding the capital of Tollan, also called Tula. According to sacred traditions taught in Aztec schools, Tollan was remembered as a kind of golden age when agricultural abundance, technological excellence, spiritual genius, and artistic perfection were united under the patronage of the great divine being, Quetzalcoatl, the Plumed Serpent, and the ruler Topiltzin Quetzalcoatl. The Aztecs looked to the Toltecs of Tollan as the inventors of culture and the apex of human and spiritual experience. They were

> very wise. Their works were all good, all perfect, all wonderful, all miraculous, their houses beautiful, tiled in mosaics, smooth stuccoed, very marvelous.[29]

They not only had wonderful ceremonial centers but also created the calendar, "originated the year count, they established the way in which the night, the day would work . . . they discerned the orbits of the stars"[30] and invented the rituals of divination and healing. We know of course that these cultural patterns were invented and elaborated during the millennium prior to the Toltec kingdom, but the Aztecs continually drew their

prestige from this fabulous memory. In fact, so important was this human Quetzalcoatl to the Aztecs that they proclaimed: "Truly with him it began, truly from him it flowed out, from Quetzalcoatl — all art and knowledge."[31]

One of the reasons for this prestige was the career of the priest-king. According to the over fifty texts, fragments, and references to Topiltzin Quetzalcoatl in the evidence, his life was permeated with sacrality, achievements, and leadership. One of the most celebrated events in this holy man's career was his personal experience and knowledge of the Creative Pair, Ometeotl, who dwelt in the innermost part of heaven at the summit of the cosmos. According to one text, Ce Acatl Quetzalcoatl (1 Reed Quetzalcoatl — another name for the hero) built a special temple facing the cardinal directions and fasted, did penance, and bathed in icy-cold waters before setting thorns into his flesh on the summits of four sacred mountains near Tollan. Then he

> sent up his prayers, his supplications into the heart of the sky and called out to Skirt of Stars, Light of Day, Lady of Sustenance, Wrapped in Coal, Wrapped in Black, She who endows the earth with solidity, He who covers the earth with cotton."[32]

Apparently his quest to communicate with the high god was successful, for "they knew that he was crying out to the place of Duality, which lies above the ninefold heaven. And thus they knew, they who dwell there, that he called upon them and petitioned them most humbly and contritely."[33]

However, the ritual career of the human Quetzalcoatl(s) appears as complex and perhaps contradictory in the record. This is particularly true in relation to the practice of human sacrifice; this hombre-dios is seen as both supporting and abandoning human sacrifice. It is possible that either a priest-king Topiltzin Quetzalcoatl of

Tollan changed during his lifetime in respect to the sacrifice of humans or the record is telling us of at least two different individuals who served as famous Quetzalcoatl priests and had different ritual approaches.

For instance, in one surviving tradition the young Topiltzin of Tollan spends seven years of ritual training to become a warrior, utilizing sacred forces to enhance his battlefield experience. He fights alongside his father, who is killed and buried in the sand by enemies. Topiltzin recovers his father's body and buries him at a shrine on Cloud Serpent Mountain and then revenges his father's death by capturing his killers and sacrificing them on the mountain before setting out to make other conquests.[34]

Yet other sources tell that Topiltzin initiated a reformation in human sacrificial practices later in his career when

> during the life of Quetzalcoatl certain sorcerers attempted to shame him into making human offerings, into sacrificing humans. But he would not consent. He would not comply, because he loved his subjects who were Toltecs. The offerings he made were only of snakes, birds, and butterflies.[35]

Then he was tricked into violating his priestly vows of sobriety and sexual abstinence by his enemy Tezcatlipoca, Lord of the Smoking Mirror, and Quetzalcoatl was forced to flee his kingdom.

The story of this flight was apparently well known to the Aztecs, who could identify in story and song the places he stopped to rest, eat, and search for ritual objects. He arrived at the celestial shore of divine waters, where he wept, discarded his ornaments, green mask, and feathers, and sacrificed himself by cremation. From his ashes emerged birds the colors of the rainbow, and "the heart of Quetzalcoatl rose to heaven, and according to the elders, was transformed into the Morning Star . . . and Quetzalcoatl was called Lord of the Dawn."[36]

In this way, Quetzalcoatl ascends into heaven to become a permanent part of celestial and calendrical *renewal* as Venus, one of the most important heavenly forces in Mesoamerican religions. It is this dimension of Quetzalcoatl's renewal and return that played a role in the third Quetzalcoatl's confusing career in Aztec history. This theme of Quetzalcoatl's celestial return was expressed, apparently in the belief that Quetzalcoatl would someday return to reclaim his throne in Tollan or one of its successors. A rare but important fragment tells that Quetzalcoatl did not die on the shore but instead sailed to the east on a raft of serpents, promising to return one day.[37]

When the forces of Cortés arrived on the edges of the Aztec world, Moctezuma sent messengers to spy on and meet the intruders and report back to him. In Sahagún's account we see that, according to Aztec elders thirty years after the conquest,

> It was as if he (Moctezuma) thought the new arrival was our prince Quetzalcoatl. This is what he felt in his heart: He has appeared! He has come back! He will come here, to the place of his throne and canopy for that is what he promised when he departed.[38]

In this controversial account, collected from the Aztec neighbors/rivals of Tlatelolco, decades after the fact, it is stated that Moctezuma in his heart and mind identified Cortés as the reappearance of Quetzalcoatl, who has returned to claim his throne as he promised. Remarkably, we have similar passages in the second letter of Hernán Cortés to the Spanish monarch Charles V where Moctezuma, *without ever mentioning Quetzalcoatl by name,* identifies Cortés or Charles V as an ancestor who departed years before and has now returned to rule. The implication of these two sources, one based on a native informant and the other on an eyewitness account, is stunning. They imply that the story of Quetzalcoatl's flight from Tula and

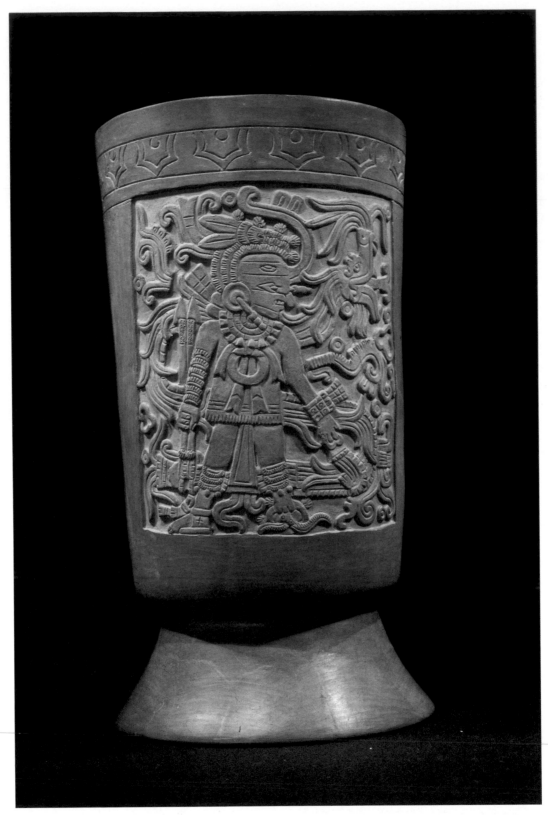

Ceramic funerary urn depicting Tezcatlipoca, from Offering 14 at the Great Temple of Tenochtitlan. Museo del Templo Mayor, México, D.F. *(Height: 13 inches.)*

promise to return played, *initially,* an important role in the Aztecs interpretation of the Spaniards.

One group of scholars has decided that this part of the Quetzalcoatl tradition, the return of Quetzalcoatl, is a postconquest invention by Spaniards and Indians who fabricated it in order to explain either the rapid fall of Tenochtitlan (in the Indian case) or the brilliant success of Cortés showing off to the king of Spain (in the Spanish case). Others, like myself, believe that it represents not a postconquest fabrication in order to explain an incredible political collapse, but a *postconquest elaboration* of an indigenous tradition. In this view there was an indigenous belief in Quetzalcoatl's return, for in the cosmovision of the Aztecs many of the gods return in periodic patterns. Further,

this view holds that the indigenous story of Quetzalcoatl's return was utilized by both Indian and Spaniard to *interpret* in different ways the catastrophe and marvel that was the fall of the world of Moctezuma. The accounts summarized above *are* postconquest but they are based on both preconquest themes and the postconquest political crisis of interpreting the agony of 1521.

And there are still people in Mexico who believe that Quetzalcoatl may yet return in another fabulous manifestation to transform the present into an idyllic past. Given this splendid career and the rich potential meanings still waiting to be deciphered, it is best, perhaps, to let the reader decide his or her view of the meaning of the Return of Quetzalcoatl.

NOTES

1. Mircea Eliade, *The Two and the One,* trans. J. M. Cohen (Chicago: University of Chicago Press, 1965), pp. 9–10.

2. Tzvetan Todorov, *The Conquest of America: The Question of the Other* (New York: Harper and Row, 1984), p. 5.

3. Bernal Díaz del Castillo, *The Discovery and Conquest of Mexico* (New York: Farrar, Straus and Giroux, 1956), p. 191.

4. Ibid.

5. Davíd Carrasco, *Quetzalcoatl and the Irony of Empire: Myths and Prophecies in the Aztec Tradition* (Chicago: University of Chicago Press, 1982), p. 1.

6. See Paul Wheatley, "City as Symbol," Inaugural Lecture delivered at the University College, London, November 20, 1967.

7. Paul Kirchhoff, "Mesoamerica," *Acta Americana* 1 (1943): 92–107.

8. See Paul Wheatley, *The Pivot of the Four Quarters: A Preliminary Enquiry into the Nature and Character of the Ancient Chinese City* (Chicago: Aldine, 1971), esp. pp. 225–369 (ch. 3).

9. Ibid.

10. Davíd Carrasco, "Toward the Splendid City: The Study of Mesoamerican Religions," *Religious Studies Review* 14 no. 4 (October 1988): 291.

11. Carlos Fuentes, *Where the Air is Clear,* trans. Sam Hileman (New York: I. Obolensky, 1960).

12. Kent Flannery, *The Early Mesoamerican Village* (New York: Academic Press, 1976).

13. Alfredo López Austin, *Hombre-Dios, Religión y Política en el Mundo Nahuatl* (México: Universidad Autónoma Nacional de México, 1973), p. 9.

14. Robert McC. Adams, *The Evolution of Urban Society* (Chicago: Aldine, 1967), p. 33.

15. Miguel León-Portilla, "The Ethnohistoric Record for the Huey Teocalli of Tenochtitlan," in *The Aztec Templo Mayor,* ed. Elizabeth Boone (Washington, D.C.: Dumbarton Oaks, 1987), p. 83.

16. Fray Bernardino de Sahagún, *The Florentine Codex: General History of the Things of New Spain, Book III,* as quoted and translated in Miguel León-Portilla, *Native Mesoamerican Spirituality* (New York: Paulist Press, 1980), pp. 220–225.

17. Lewis Henry Morgan, "Montezuma's Dinner," *North American Review* 122 (1876): 308.

18. Sahagún, *Florentine Codex: General History of the Things of New Spain, Book VII,* trans. Arthur J.O. Anderson and Charles E. Dibble (Santa Fe, N.M.: School of American Research and University of Utah, 1978), p. 26.

19. León-Portilla, *Native Mesoamerican Spirituality,* pp. 241–242.

20. Ibid., p. 243.

21. Ibid.

22. Sahagún, *Florentine Codex,* Book VI, p. 167.

23. Ibid., pp. 237–240.

24. In this section I am indebted to the work of David Damrosch

and his "The Aesthetics of Conquest: Aztec Poetry Before and After Cortés," *Representations* 33 (Winter 1991): 101–120.

25. Ibid.

26. Ibid.

27. Ibid.

28. Sahagún, *Florentine Codex,* Book III, p. 39.

29. Ibid., Book X, p. 166.

30. Ibid., p. 168.

31. *Anales de Cuauhtitlán,* quoted in León-Portilla, *Native Mesoamerican Spirituality,* p. 169.

32. Ibid.

33. Ibid.

34. *Leyenda de los Soles,* quoted in John Bierhorst, *Four Masterworks of American Indian Literature* (New York: Farrar, Straus and Giroux, 1974), p. 21.

35. *Anales de Cuauhtitlán,* quoted in León-Portilla, *Native American Spirituality,* p. 29.

36. Ibid., p. 62.

37. The best work on the Topiltzin Quetzalcoatl tradition was accomplished by H. B. Nicholson in "The Topiltzin Quetzalcoatl of Tollan Tale: A Problem in Mesoamerican Ethnohistory" (Ph.D. diss., Harvard University, 1957).

38. Quoted in Miguel León-Portilla, *The Broken Spears: Aztec Account of the Conquest of Mexico* (Boston: Beacon Press, 1961), p. 23.

MOCTEZUMA'S SKY: AZTEC ASTRONOMY AND RITUAL

ANTHONY F. AVENI

ASTRONOMY: THE WRITTEN AND UNWRITTEN RECORD

When we think of astronomy we conjure up images of a vast limitless universe of galaxies, warped space-time, and black holes. We think of space-based telescopes and the search for extraterrestrials. Our textbooks teach us that astronomy is but one of many branches of experimental science. Its means are mathematical precision, careful observations and record keeping, its ends knowledge for its own sake — to know what makes the universe tick. The Aztecs were astute stargazers, too. But to understand them we must divorce ourselves totally from all of these modern impressions.

There are some revealing statements written by the Spanish chroniclers on the subject of Aztec skywatching. For example, Torquemada describes the celestial exploits of the king of Tezcoco, one Nezahualpilli, as follows:

They say he was a great astrologer and prided himself much on his knowledge of the motions of the celestial bodies; and being attached to this study, that he caused inquiries to be made throughout the entire extent of his dominions, for all such persons as were at all conversant with it, whom he brought to his court, and imparted to them whatever he knew, and ascending by night on the terraced roof of his palace, he thence considered the stars, and disputed with them on all different questions connected with them.[1]

Then he goes on to describe the king's observatory. It was a walled enclosure situated on the roof of the palace with just enough room for the king to lie down in. There he would peep through (or over) a device Torquemada describes as "a lance, upon which was hung a sphere. And I think that the reason of the walls being elevated one yard above the terrace, and a sphere of cotton or silk being hung from the poles, was for the sake of measuring more exactly the celestial motions." What did the astronomer-king look at? How was he measuring? And what was served by the data collected?

Because Torquemada wrote his chronicle nearly a century after the conquest (he obtained all this information from the king's last surviving grandson) and because he himself knew little about astronomy, it is difficult to know what to make of his tantalizing statements. We can be sure, however, that this king knew all about the skies over Tezcoco and what they portended for all the inhabitants of the Valley of Mexico. So widespread was his knowledge that, according to another chronicler, he was called upon to advise the most

149

A great comet viewed from the roof of the king's palace. Was it the one said to have predicted the fall of the empire of Moctezuma? From the *Codex Durán,* Museo Nacional de Antropología, México, D.F.

famous king of all. Father Diego Durán tells of the appearance of a great comet said to have presaged the fall of Tenochtitlan.

> Moctezuma, having observed the comet since midnight, went the next day to Netzahualpilli to seek its meaning. Replied the king of Tezcoco, "Your vassals, the astrologers, soothsayers and diviners have been careless! That sign in the heavens has been there for some time and yet you describe it to me now as if it were a new thing. I thought you had already discovered it and that your astrologers had explained it to you. Since you now tell me you have seen it I will answer you that that brilliant star appeared in the heavens many days ago."[2]

He goes on to give details of the frightful omens of disasters that indeed later befell the unfortunate monarch. If it seems odd to the reader to find the occult art of astrology wedded to scientific astronomy, keep in mind that until well after the West European Renaissance the principal reason to follow the course of the stars was to interpret messages that celestial spirits sent to us here on earth. All over the world human thought and action have been intimately tied to events that transpire in the heavens. As the Babylonian cuneiform tablets in the Old World and the Maya codices in the New World demonstrate, precise, mathematically correct predictions about the positions of celestial bodies are generated out of religious concerns.

Moctezuma himself seems to have supervised a phase in the construction of the Templo Mayor with a basic astronomical principle in mind. The chronicler Motolinía tells of a festival dedicated to the flaying of prisoners (in which the priests dressed themselves in the skins of their captives). He tells us that the event took place at the beginning of the spring season "when the sun was in the middle of [the temple of] Huitzilopochtli, which was the equinox, and because this was a little twisted, Moctezuma wished it torn down and straightened."[3] Today the unwritten record confirms the general truth of Motolinía's statement. Archaeological investigation reveals that the building lines up exactly with the rising sun on March 21, but this event does not take place in the

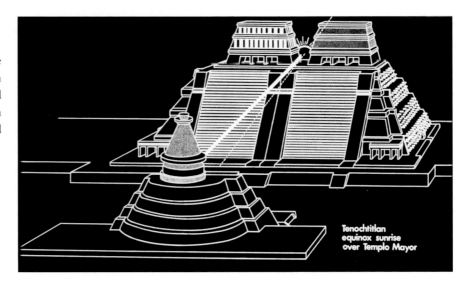

Sunrise over the Great Temple. The dotted line shows the path of the sun as it becomes elevated to its intended position in the notch between the twin temples. (Mesoamerican Archive and Research Project.)

Tenochtitlan equinox sunrise over Templo Mayor

direction of due east as we might expect. If you go to the plaza in front of the temple to watch the sun rise at the equinoxes, you will note that it moves slowly to the right (south of east) as it ascends. It will not appear over the top of the temple (or the notch in between the twin temples of Tlaloc and Huitzilopochtli) until it is situated nearly 7 degrees south of east. This is precisely the direction in which we find the temple skewed today.

MARKING TIME BY SUN AND STARS

Marking time seems to be the major concern in the exercise we just described. King Moctezuma had apparently been grappling with the rather difficult problem of bringing the precise time to conduct a ritual into the correct space — the space in front of the Great Temple where the rituals were to be enacted. That he succeeded is a tribute to his advisors' knowledge of both engineering and astronomy.

As we might expect from a highly organized state, Aztec ritual practice seems to be imbued with the idea of doing things in the proper place at the appropriate time. We know they began each fifty-two-year calendar round precisely when the Pleiades crossed the fifth cardinal point or the

zenith of heaven at midnight (this happened in mid-November). Priests ascended the Hill of the Star, a hilltop on a peninsula that juts out into the very middle of the lake, to mark the event. In Chapter 6 of his *General History of the Things of New Spain,* the Franciscan friar Bernardino de Sahagún identifies the Pleiades as Tianquiztli, the Marketplace. Perhaps the compactness of this star cluster is reminiscent of the crowded nature of the Aztec marketplace? He pictures them among certain astronomical phenomena and other, as yet unidentified, Aztec constellations. This important constellation appears to have figured in the king's inauguration ceremony. On the night of his ascent to the throne he was exhorted (among other religious duties) to arise at midnight and look at the stars that precisely mark the four cardinal points of the sky: at *Yohualitqui Mamalhuaztli* (the sticks with which fire is drilled), the *Citlaltlachtli* (a celestial ball court possibly identified with Gemini, the Twins), at *Colotl Ixayac* (the Scorpion, which may be the same as that of Western star lore), and, of course, at Tianquiztli (Tezozomoc).

It is interesting that all of these star groups lie on the zodiac and therefore could have served as time markers to chart the motion of the sun, moon, and planets that move along that roadway of stars. This habit of using sky events as temporal

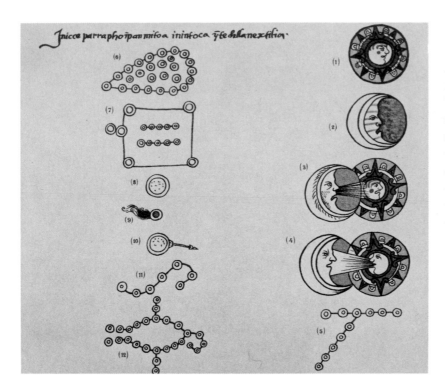

Aztec constellations from Sahagún's *Primeros Memoriales* (after Paso y Troncoso). The sun, moon, and eclipses are obvious, as is the smoking star (a meteor or shooting star). Tianquiztli (the Pleiades) is at the upper left, below which the celestial ball-court (Gemini?) is located. Among the other constellations are the sticks one uses to drill fire, lower right, which correspond to the belt and sword of our Orion.

Sky events number the pages of Aztec history. For example, our year 1509 (written in Spanish gloss at the top) corresponds to the Aztec year defined by the Year Bearer 4 House (the name of the New Year's Day for that year). *Codex Telleriano-Remensis,* Bibliothèque Nationale, Paris, France.

indicators is exhibited in frame after frame of the surviving codices from central Mexico, where we see battles, accessions, and alliances pictorially represented and labeled above by specific dates and natural (often astronomical) events. For example, the appearance of smoking stars *(citlalin popoca)* is often depicted. We have not sorted which of these might have been comets or meteors — even meteoritic falls, also called star excrement. (The German ethnologist Ulrich Köhler reports that contemporary Nahua people of the mountains of Veracruz believe a close relationship exists between meteors and caterpillars. When a meteorite arrives on earth they say that black caterpillars appear. When heaped together in one's hand these *citlalocuile* or star-caterpillars look like *citlalcuitlatl,* star excrement.) Other depictions of natural events in the codices include eclipses, even an occasional snowstorm.

Although we have difficulty specifying precisely which astronomical object is cited, the framework of time that depicts the important events of Aztec history is always marked by both a calendrical date and a natural event. Unlike the more abstract Maya hieroglyphic calendar, for the Aztecs the world of nature, revealed pictorially, seems very much a part of the way to express human history.

ASTRONOMICAL TIME AND RITUAL SPACE

Many of the traditions of Aztec Tenochtitlan frighten us — its warlike imperialism, the practice of human sacrifice on a large scale, priests wearing the skins of their captives. The evidence we have been looking at helps us to realize that our fascination, even our overt condemnation of these people is worthy of some deeper reconsideration. It seems clear that the Aztecs were very careful observers of nature and that they used the sky to fashion a precise system of astronomy as well as a complex, never-ending calendar composed of cycle built upon carefully timed cycle all the way up to the five cycles of creation that we see depicted on their famous Calendar Stone.

It is here and in other Aztec monumental sculpture and works of architecture, strategically placed around the ancient capital, that we discover a key that unlocks the doorway between precise astronomy and timekeeping, which we seem all too willing to try to understand, and that elusive Aztec ideology, which we have such difficulty comprehending. The cityscape and the skyscape join at the doorway of Aztec mythology. That doorway is entered when we begin to perceive the way people used Tenochtitlan's stage to act out the purpose of their creation — to conduct their rituals. The rounds of time, from the naming of the days of the short cycle of the Aztec week to the long cycles of destruction and re-creation, are framed in stone. They serve as a mandate to the people. The images of the flint-tongued sun god Tonatiuh at the center of the Calendar Stone is a reminder to all good citizens that their purpose is to keep the world going, to nourish the sun god with life's blood that he might ever continue upon his celestial rounds, never to become extinguished by the threatening powers of eternal darkness.

The cylindrical shape of Tizoc's stone encapsulates the very reason for the existence of the military state. As art historian Richard Townsend has shown, it depicts one of Moctezuma's predecessors in action upon life's stage, sandwiched quite legitimately in between the world of subterranean nature below and the sky above. (See page 30.) "We are gathering up the vital fluid to nurture our gods and to keep the heavens in motion," the stone seems to say to the people. In addition to cycles carved in stone, monthly and yearly rounds also took place continually throughout the space of the city all the way out to the environment of its periphery.

To give an example of an astronomically timed

153

The Tizoc Stone, commemorating the conquests of Tizoc, the seventh Aztec tlatoani. Museo Nacional de Antropología, México, D.F. *(Diameter: 68 inches; height: 26 inches.)*

Atop Mt. Tlaloc is an enclosure fifty meters on a side with a 125-meter-long walled access way that aligns precisely with the direction to the Templo Mayor, as if to invoke a dialogue between the rain god, who calls up rain from the interior of his mountain home, and the people who pay their debt to him in the center of the city. Here, too, intricate sunwatching is implicated: the causeway, misaligned from the sides of the enclosure, also lines up with the place where the sun sets twenty days before a great feast honoring Tlaloc at his birthplace in the Aztec month of Huey Tozoztli. (Mesoamerican Archive and Research Project.)

ritual that evokes the ideology of the Aztec state, let us return to center stage, the Templo Mayor, and assemble some actors: Moctezuma's priests who ministered to the ritual of debt payment to the rain god, Tlaloc, and the children with special day names whom the priests selected to be led to certain mountaintops that ring the Valley of Mexico. There they would be sacrificed to Tlaloc. The time is the first twenty-day month of the Aztec year, Atlcahualo, which ran from February 12 to March 4. Sahagún describes what happened: "And if the children went crying, if their tears kept flowing, if their tears kept falling, it was said, it was

stated: 'It will surely rain.' Their tears signified rain. Therefore there was contentment; therefore one's heart was at rest. Thus they said: 'Verily, already the rains will set in; verily, already we shall be rained on.' And if one who was dropsical was somewhere, 'There is no rain for us.' "[4]

Today we can use the chronicler's statements, together with modern maps and extant place-names, to determine most of the locations cited in the ritual. When we lay these places out on a modern map of Mexico City, we discover two principles of order buried in the chronicler's description of the sites. First, these places fall in

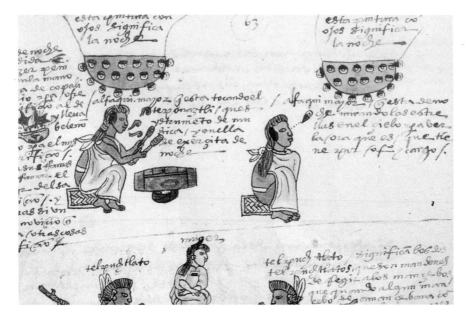

An Aztec town crier beats on his *teponaztli* to announce the hours of the night, which he has determined by watching the stars, page 63 of the *Codex Mendoza*.

clockwise order around the lake basin, and second, the sequence begins at a mountaintop shrine called Quauhtepetl that lines up precisely on the extension of the northern axis of the city. Why start in the north? Perhaps it was because north was conceived as the entrance to the underworld, a pan-Mesoamerican belief reflected in the association of the north-south axis with the up-down direction. At Teotihuacan, the place of birth of the Aztec gods, there is a mountain on the north that influenced the orientation of that ancient city as well. Another of the sites in the Atlcahualo ritual, Tepetzinco, is the little hill just outside the entrance to Mexico City's airport. Then it was an island in the middle of the lake and it served as another place of deposition of the precious debt payment to Tlaloc for bringing rain. The direction to this island held astronomical significance. It bears 7 degrees south of east from the Templo Mayor at a radial distance of five kilometers. This marks the place where the sun rose twenty days after the vernal or twenty days before the autumnal equinox. Now the hills of the Tlaloc range, where Tlalocan, the home of the rain god, is located lie 7 degrees north of east. They mark the course of the rising sun during the twenty-day month *before* the vernal equinox, as viewed from

the Templo Mayor. Sacred space and sacred time seem to intersect in this aspect of the ritual. In other words, in the solar orientation calendar employed by the Mexica state the strategic little island of Tepetzinco, where all the children were held before the beginning of the ritual, may have served to define the time one Mesoamerican month on the opposite side of the equinox relative to that indicated by Tlaloc's mountain range, as seen from the Templo Mayor.

The selection of the sixth site, Cocotl, is less interesting from a calendrical or geographical than from a politically strategic point of view. It lies well out of the center of the Valley on the southeast trade route in the territory of the Chalcans, long-time enemies of Tenochtitlan who only late in preconquest history were brought under Aztec hegemony.

Today this place can be identified with a mountain in the modern village of Cocotitlan. The remains of a pyramid and late Aztec pottery sherds in great abundance still adorn its summit.

Another deposition point in the Atlcahualo ritual is of special interest because it is located on the mountain skyline just above the shrine of Guadalupe, the site of the miracle of 1531. Could this place, called Yoaltecatl by Sahagún, have been

156

Teponaxtli. Red ceramic horizontal drum, Museo Nacional de Antropología, México, D.F. *(Length: 24 inches.)*

an indigenous antecedent of the sacred place adopted by Christian worshippers? The summit is a flat area several hectares in extent located northeast of the Templo Mayor. At least one ruined pyramidal structure and the remains of several other platforms are situated there, but much of the building stone has been repositioned in the construction of cattle pens and field boundaries by the small but ever-increasing population of peasants who now dwell there.

Many questions about the Atlcahualo ritual still confound us. Did celebrants go out and come back all at once, or was each part of the ritual conducted in temporal order? Did the procession move repeatedly to and from the center or did it proceed in one continuous sweep in a clockwise direction about the horizon? Going out and returning to the center may have functioned as a symbolic act of repeatedly pulling in the edges of the city toward its center. Did different people perform different parts of these rituals as part of a

mechanism for social cohesion? Were these far-flung sites marked out in the ritual landscape only once a year, in the month of Atlcahualo? And why begin the year in February rather than at the solstice or equinox as so many other cultures have done? Indeed, we begin ours at a solstice! Perhaps, as Davíd Carrasco has suggested, the opening of the ritual period (Month No. 1) of the Mexica year would be the most appropriate time to cosmicize and domesticate space through pilgrimage in a large number of diverse directions. The sacrifice of young children is one logical means of initiating Tlaloc's cosmic power. Here was the ultimate divine-human exchange. Thus did the state synthesize and map out, in abbreviated form, the whole ceremonial landscape in the month just before the rainy season.

We are a long way from being in the skins of the Aztecs, from knowing the meaning behind their rites, the truth as they conceived it about their myths. But we do know that astronomy, calendar-keeping and environmental considerations came together not in just scheduling the time to conduct a ritual but also in ordering the places in which to conduct it. And there were also considerations about the relationship between conqueror and tributary, center and periphery.

We cannot understand Aztec skywatching without also being forced to gain insight into the way Tenochtitlan sought to integrate cosmic harmony with the social-political harmony they believed must exist among tribute towns, ethnic groups, and the vertical strata of society.

The "town crier" who chanted out the hours, the priests who watched the Pleiades pass overhead, the twenty-day calendar units written in the codices, the sun seen rising over the temple — all of these images stress the practical side of Aztec time-ordering that rests upon a foundation of careful observation of nature. This was Aztec astronomy. And we can appreciate how King Moctezuma must have struggled with the problem of

integrating concepts of architecture, horizon astronomy, and fixing points of pilgrimage to fit into a calendar. Astronomy was one of many interlocking means to an ideological end. It helped to voice the ideology of a tiny city-state that blossomed to a vast empire literally moments before the European intrusion.

Eduardo Matos has aptly interpreted the juxtaposition of the twin temples atop the Templo Mayor — one to the rain god, the other to the god of the sun and war — as a statement of the resoundingly successful ideology of the Aztec state. There agrarian interests and the militarism of the new expansionist state converge. We witness the same sort of convergence when we map out the ritual of Atlcahualo, and the astronomers who watched Moctezuma's sky were there to record and interpret events that foretold of the harmony or disharmony that might ensue from the celestial order to which King Moctezuma and his friend Nezahualpilli paid rapt attention.

NOTES

1. Juan de Torquemada, *Monarquía Indiana,* Vol. 1, Book 2 (1723 edition), ch. 44, p. 188.

2. Fray Diego Durán, *The Aztecs: The History of the Indies of New Spain,* trans. Doris Heyden and Fernando Horcasitas (London: Cassell, 1964), pp. 247–248.

3. Fray Toribio de Benavente Motolinía, *History of the Indians of New Spain* (Washington, D.C.: Academy of American Franciscan History, 1951).

4. Fray Bernardino de Sahagún, *Florentine Codex: General History of the Things of New Spain, Book II,* trans. Arthur J.O. Anderson and Charles E. Dibble (Santa Fe, N.M.: School of American Research and University of Utah, 1978).

GLORIOUS IMPERIUM: UNDERSTANDING LAND AND COMMUNITY IN MOCTEZUMA'S MEXICO

ELIZABETH HILL BOONE

WISDOM IN THE PAINTED BOOKS

Shortly after the Spanish adventurer Hernán Cortés and some five hundred conquistadores set foot on the Gulf Coast of Veracruz on Good Friday, 1519, to begin the Spanish invasion of Mexico, they were greeted by the Indian governor of that region. As Bernal Díaz del Castillo, a lieutenant of Cortés, reported, the governor "brought with him some clever painters such as they had in Mexico and ordered them to make pictures true to nature of the face and body of Cortés and all his captains, and of the soldiers, ships, sails and horses, and of Doña Marina and [the Spaniard] Aguilar [interpreters whom Cortés acquired earlier], even two greyhounds, and the cannon and cannon balls, and all of the army we had brought with us."[1] These paintings the native governor had rushed overland to the Aztec emperor Moctezuma, who controlled most of what is now called Mesoamerica from his magnificent island capital of Tenochtitlan, now Mexico City.

The artists were *tlacuillos,* to use the Aztec term of the Nahuatl language. They were manuscript painters or scribes, who recorded pictographically and glyphically the religion, calendars, prophecies, histories, and economic matters of the Aztec em-

pire. Their paintings of Cortés and his party enabled Moctezuma to assess the nature, if not the intent and ultimate threat, of this European intrusion.

Mesoamerica (which extends from northern Mexico down into Central America as far as northwestern Honduras and El Salvador) was unique among all the cultural areas of the Americas because its people developed graphic writing systems to record knowledge, and they created manuscripts or books to contain the writings and paintings. The Aztec writing system was not alphabetic, as is ours, nor did it replicate spoken language by presenting a series of words tied together into sentences and paragraphs. Instead its message went more directly to the mind of the reader, without a detour through speech. The reader of Aztec writing saw and received a combination of naturalistic images, pictorial conventions, abstract symbols, and hieroglyphs that were painted within an organized structure. By knowing the basic conventions and the meanings of the symbols, and by recognizing how they were arranged on the painted page, he or she could understand the message. Of course, the more esoteric and layered the symbolic meaning of the images, the more difficult was the precise interpretation or reading. Pictorial writing was enormously old in Mesoamerica. The

The *Codex Féjérváry-Mayer,* a screenfold book of deerhide painted to record divinatory almanacs and descriptions of ceremonies. Page 1 is a cosmogram representing the four world directions. (After *Codex Féjérváry-Mayer,* intro. C. A. Burland. Graz: Academische Druck und Verlagsanstalt, 1971 facsimile edition.)

first hieroglyphs were invented as early as 1000 B.C., and the first books may have been fashioned then, too.

The painted books served as a specialized means of communication among the elite of the Aztec empire: the priests, rulers, and high government officials who could interpret the images and, on ceremonial occasions, would expand them into long and elaborate oral recitations. If we can judge by the distribution of scribes in the early Colonial period, when each town had a notary to serve the largely illiterate population, manuscript painters were similarly employed by each Aztec community. As Bartolomé de Las Casas, the first Christian bishop of Chiapas, remarked, "There was never a

lack of these manuscript painters, for the position passed from father to son; and it was a highly esteemed career in government. The rulers and priests and nobles consulted the pictorial manuscripts concerning uncertainties that arose about the ceremonies and precepts of religion, and the feasts and the gods, and in any matters of ancient government and secular matters of importance."[2]

The books or manuscripts themselves were made from panels of deer hide or paper, glued together to form a long strip. The paper was a refined bark cloth made by soaking and then pounding thin the inner bark of the native fig tree. Then the strip was most often folded screenfold- or accordion-style and primed on both sides with a fine lime sizing to form the smooth white surface on which the scribes would paint with a fine brush. When closed, the screenfolds look much like a European book, with wooden covers attached at the front and back. They were spread out flat when being read. These screenfolds were the form most commonly used, but the scribes also chose to paint their message on single panels of hide or paper, and on large cotton sheets that the Spaniards called *lienzos* (from the Spanish word for linen).

Painted calendars, astronomical tables, and divinatory almanacs guided the Aztec people through life, showing them when to plant and harvest, when to journey, when to conduct war. Other manuals outlined how ceremonies should be performed and what rites should be conducted. Dynastic histories and genealogies preserved the stories of large and powerful families. Town and city histories spoke of the settling and control of community lands. Grander histories recorded the official story of the Aztec empire. Painted accounts of tax and tribute kept tally of the great variety of goods and services owed to Moctezuma, and maps led the way across unfamiliar ground. In the fifth letter Cortés wrote to the emperor Charles V describing the invasion and conquest of Mexico, the conqueror remarked on the accuracy of Aztec maps, which showed towns, hills, rivers, swamps, and even streams, and were reliable even outside the boundaries of the empire.[3]

The painted books pervaded all aspects of Aztec life. Few have survived the intervening five centuries, but more than any other archaeological or historical resource the manuscripts of the Aztec empire speak to us directly about the Aztec mind. The armload of books that still exist from pre-Hispanic Mexico, as well as the several hundred manuscripts painted by Aztecs and written by Aztecs and Spaniards in the early Colonial period after the invasion, reveal what the Aztecs thought about themselves and their land. They help us to know how Moctezuma conceived of his empire in terms of land and space and what place he imagined his capital city of Tenochtitlan within it.

LAND AND COMMUNITY

From the early manuscripts and writings, we know that the Aztecs saw their populated world as being organized into many distinct and fairly autonomous communities. Ruled by noble families, these communities were composed of a principal nucleated settlement, smaller subject towns and hamlets, and the lands between and around that were held communally by the people. In ancient Mexico there was not the distinction between urban and rural, except perhaps with respect to the few largest cities. Cities and towns and their countryside were unified, conceptualized together within a single unit. Politically these units functioned as community kingdoms, similar to the ancient Greek city-states, that had their separate identities and fundamental independence. The people identified themselves according to their community, so that one was a Tenochca from Tenochtitlan, or a Xochimilca from the rich chinampa city of Xochimilco at the southern end of the lake region, or a Malinalca from the sentinel city of Malinalco high in the hills southwest of Tenochtitlan. Many of these community kingdoms became large and powerful, with their nucleus growing into a great city that exerted control over others, but even then the smaller community kingdoms retained their separate identity.

The conceptual reality of this system of settlement and society is reflected in the Nahuatl language spoken throughout Aztec Mexico, just as it is in the pictorial manuscripts. The word for city or town, or more appropriately for community kingdom, was *altepetl*, the word being a combination of *atl*, or "water," and *tepetl*, or "hill." This combination of water and hill is an obvious and direct reference to the need for water and land in

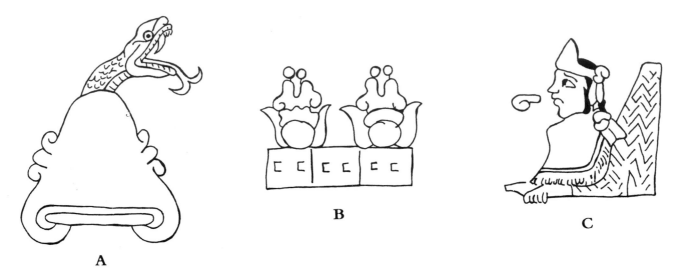

A **B** **C**

Examples of Aztec place signs and the tlatoani ruler of such a place: *a.* Coatepec, or Serpent Hill; *b.* Xochimilco, or Place of the Fields of Flowers; *c.* the tlatoani.

each community, but it also carries the deeper, metaphorical reference to the great mythical hill from which the earth's waters flow, the source of all fertility.[4]

Pictorially the altepetls are identified in the Aztec manuscripts by hieroglyphs that signal and name the place. Many of the place glyphs or place signs have as their principal element the pictorial convention for hill: a green mound whose bottom ends curl around the edges of its yellow and red base. To this, the images that characterize the polity's name are added — for example, a serpent (called *coatl*) added to the hill symbol (tepetl) identifies Coatepec, or Hill of the Serpent. Other place signs simply combine images from a community's name: Xochimilco, the Place of the Fields of Flowers, is composed of conventionalized flowers (xochitl) growing from a distinctive band that represents a plowed or worked field (milli).

The noble rulers of these communities carried the title tlatoani, literally "speaker," for not only were they the voice for their people, but they were especially skilled in oration. Visually they appear in the painted books seated on a reed mat or a throne, wrapped in a cloak, and with a speech scroll curling outward from their mouth, to signal

their status. All the rulers of altepetl communities held the title of tlatoani, regardless of how large or how small their population was. Even the great Moctezuma, who controlled the vast Aztec empire, was a tlatoani, except that he was further distinguished by being a *huey tlatoani,* or great speaker.

Throughout Mexico before — and even for a few centuries after — the Spanish invasion of 1519, the community kingdoms identified themselves and defined their physical extent in paintings on broad panels of cotton cloth. These lienzos are maps or diagrams of a community and its communal lands painted together with historical and genealogical information about the ruling family. Every city-state or community kingdom seems to have had one, for they not only served as land titles, but they conveyed the community's fundamental identity; they located the community both in space and in time. All the surviving lienzos date from after the Spanish conquest, but they recall pre-Columbian antecedents. Two examples, the Lienzo de Tequixtepec and the Lienzo de Zacatepec, show what kinds of information these town charters recorded and how it was arranged and presented.

The Lienzo de Tequixtepec (photo courtesy of Ross Parmenter).

The small town of Tequixtepec, in the Coixtla-huaca Valley of northern Oaxaca, has guarded its great lienzo since it was painted in the late six-teenth century. The painting came to the attention of historians only in the 1970s, when a boundary dispute with a neighbor compelled the town to seek outside advice on using the lienzo for evi-dence. A Mexico City lawyer has said he could settle the dispute once and for all if the town would let him take their lienzo to the capital city and present it in court. But since other villages had lost their lienzos once the paintings were in Mex-ico City, Tequixtepec ultimately decided to send photographs instead, and the town still retains its lienzo.[5]

Measuring about ten by seven feet, the lienzo has more color than most. On its rough cloth surface the territorial extent of the community is visually detailed in a conceptualized geography. Tequixtepec is pictured in the center by its large place sign, a green conventionalized hill (tepetl) in which is a *tecciztli* shell, providing the phonetic reading of the town's name — *teccizt* and *tepec*. Instead of a single tlatoani ruler, the two couples who founded Tequixtepec sit facing each other on the jaguar thrones that are the symbol of rulership. Generously spaced around them are the place signs and rulers of dependencies or subject towns; a river runs from top to bottom on the left of the conventionalized map, and the whole is bordered by a rectangular frame that is spotted with the place glyphs that defined Tequixtepec's boundary. Although these individual boundary signs have not been interpreted, usually such boundary markers are towns, fields, or special topographic features such as boulders or springs; often they are arranged roughly according to their actual geo-graphic location. Together these features establish the geographic and the political definition of Tequixtepec.

The place of Tequixtepec in mythical and historical time is explained visually below the map.

There, in two rows of rectangular frames spanning the width of the sheet, are portrayals of the twenty-five ancestral couples who are important to Tequixtepec's history. Below this still, the people's creation legend is painted in the panels of three more broad registers.

As a whole, the lienzo presents Tequixtepec's community identity. Principally it names the pol-ity and defines its geographical situation; then it names its rulers, presents their claim or right to rule by giving their genealogy, and carries the line back fully to the point of origin.

Turning now to the lienzo of the coastal town of Zacatepec, we see most of the same features, differently arranged.[6] Where Tequixtepec's lienzo was colored, the Lienzo de Zacatepec, like many others, was painted only with black. Less symmet-rical and static in its representation, it is more visually complex, with history actually overlaid on the geographic foundation. Again, a cartographic rectangle, regularly patterned with the place signs of the boundaries, defines Zacatepec's territory, and the town itself is signaled by the largest and most elaborate place sign, centrally located toward the top of the sheet. The rivers are shown, one flowing up from the bottom of the map. Here and there within the rectangle are the place glyphs and rulers of subject towns as well as the glyphs of some uninhabited locations. Zacatepec's territory is presented in such a manner as Tequixtepec's, but its history is differently structured.

Less rigidly genealogical, Zacatepec's lienzo details the history of three generations of Za-catepec rulers, from their arrival into the area to their conquest and accommodation of neighbor-ing peoples. Instead of putting this in a separate section of the cloth sheet, however, it lays the historical narrative directly over the original car-tographic base. The story begins in the upper left corner, outside the boundary of Zacatepec, where the founder of the local dynasty receives political authority from a great eleventh-century ruler. The

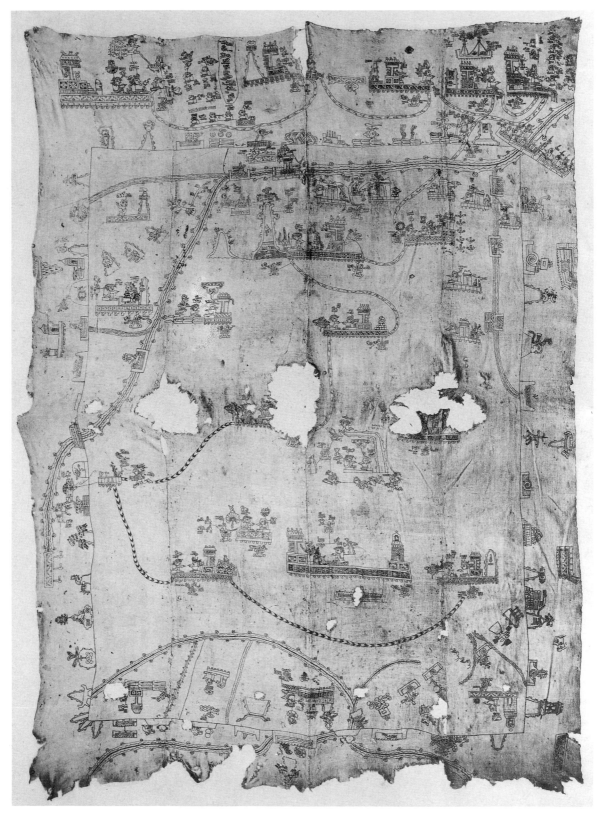

The Lienzo de Zacatepec (after Antonio Peñafiel, *Códice Mixteco: Lienzo de Zacatepec,* México: Secretaría de Fomento, 1900).

founder then makes a pilgrimage across the top of the cloth to the far right and finally enters the boundary of Zacatepec, where he establishes his rule and is presented seated facing his wife. Paths of footprints mark the progression. After this point the founder is no longer an important character in the story, and the narrative moves to the left, to the next generation of rulers, who are shown in the upper center of the map seated as a couple on an elaboration of the Zacatepec place glyph. They also then drop from the narrative, which picks up the third-generation ruler and his conquests that consolidate the Zacatepec domain.

The Lienzo de Zacatepec and the Lienzo de Tequixtepec were both painted to identify their community kingdoms; and the identity of these communities was conceived in temporal as well as spatial terms. The first concern of the lienzos was to describe the territorial extent of the community with its communal lands and to set these apart from their neighbors'. These were agricultural communities whose land-based economies demanded a careful accounting and secure claiming of lands; it was, and remains, essential to know where one's fields, watershed, and hunting territory began and ended. After this was set, it was important to locate the community temporally with respect to its past and its genealogical lineage — to fix the community in time and also to present the credentials of its ruling family to govern. Some lienzos, like the Tequixtepec, painted the historical information beside the map, and others, like the Zacatepec, wound the historical narrative through the geographic features.

For preconquest peoples without an alphabetic writing system, lienzos functioned as a community charter and survey. Since the conquest they have successfully served this same purpose for nearly four hundred years. The Spanish courts accepted lienzos as valid land titles in the Colonial period, as do Mexican courts today. More than valid titles, however, villages guard their lienzos,

perhaps the way churches guard their relics, as paintings that embody community, and largely Indian, identity.

THE CITY AT THE CENTER OF THE WORLD, IN THE MIDDLE OF TIME

If minor villages like Zacatepec had elaborate lienzos, what would a metropolitan center like Tenochtitlan have had? It may have had a city charter of some kind that was perhaps cartographically based, but it is certain that a single lienzo could not have encompassed all the pertinent geographic and historical data for the imperial capital. In the two hundred years following its official founding, the island city of Tenochtitlan grew to one of the largest and most densely populated of all New World polities, with about 150,000 inhabitants on the island alone surrounded by approximately 1 million in the surrounding valley around the lake. Its rulers controlled the Triple Alliance that formed the Aztec empire, and they dominated all of civilized Mesoamerica, receiving tribute from as far away as Guatemala. Architecturally and sculpturally, the city expressed itself as the geographic center of the cosmos, with the Templo Mayor as world navel, or *axis mundi*.

Its manuscript needs were clearly different from those of villages like Zacatepec. The Aztecs of Tenochtitlan were less concerned with precise geographic delineation, for the empire did not have hard boundaries in the same way that Zacatepec had community borders. Rather Moctezuma's empire was composed of a series of alliances, political and military obligations, and tribute arrangements owed by the provinces to the capital. Thus, the painted books of the metropolis ignored cartography to focus on locating the Aztecs and their capital city of Tenochtitlan ideally at the center first of time and then implicitly of space. For this, they divided their history into two great narratives: one devoted to their migration and the other to their imperial rise and expansion. Then they developed a distinctive form for arranging and organizing the stories according to the continuous count of the years.

This characteristic Aztec way of organizing history is like an annal. Time is the organizing principle. All the years, whether or not anything momentous happened during them, are painted in a sequence across the wide pages of the books. The individual years appear as square cartouches that are individually designated by the numbers 1 through 13 and the signs Flint, House, Rabbit, and Reed. The count goes 1 Flint, 2 House, 3 Rabbit, 4 Reed, 5 Flint, and so forth. In the historical manuscripts the years are generally painted in a single straight line that runs usually from left to right, although sometimes they are condensed into blocks. In all cases the file of years provides the structure for the pictorial history, with the symbols for notable events painted around or directly attached to individual years. These events and actions included natural and climatic phenomena (such as eclipses, floods, and droughts), the accession to office and death of rulers, the migrations of peoples, the founding of cities, wars and conquests, ritually or mythically important events, and the like. The location of events is assumed — it is assumed to be the place of residence of the people for whom the history is painted — unless an event occurs in another locale, in which case the place sign is given. The locations of conquests or of stops along a migration, for example, are always identified by their place signs.

The Aztecs saw their history as being composed of two distinct and contrasting periods. The first was the time prior to the establishment of their capital, during which they migrated from a mythical homeland and into central Mexico. The following period is characterized by their imperial expansion and rise as the greatest military and economic power in Mesoamerica.

Aztec migration histories were painted to locate Tenochtitlan temporally at the end of a great period of hardship and wandering. The Aztecs presented themselves as a poor but fierce band, forced by their patron god Huitzilopochtli to leave the island paradise of Aztlan for new lands and a greater destiny. In one of the painted history books, the *Codex Mexicanus,* history and time begin together at Aztlan. A crowd of Aztec men and women go forth from Aztlan, presented as the place of reeds and herons. When they leave, they literally step up on the year count, which starts in the year 1 Flint (erroneously dated as the year 1168 by a later Spanish writer). From this auspicious beginning they migrate for a half dozen generations, eventually moving into the Valley of Mexico where they attempt repeatedly to settle. After being driven about by the peoples already occupying the valley, they finally make their home on a swampy island in the middle of Lake Tezcoco.

The founding of Tenochtitlan culminates the migration portion of the Aztec story and begins the imperial half. Visually the founding moment is represented by the great nopal cactus that grows from a rock on the swampy island, which is the place sign of Tenochtitlan. In the painted histories the rock and cactus combination is generally elaborated, however. In the *Codex Mexicanus* it is accompanied by the hieroglyphs for the clan groups that survived the migration to found the capital, but in other sources it bears the great eagle of their god Huitzilopochtli foretold would be perched there.

From this moment at Tenochtitlan, Aztec imperial history continues for over two hundred years, well through the coming of the Spaniards. Some imperial histories, like the *Codex Mendoza,* concentrate on the victories of the Aztec emperors; it lists the years on the left, pictures the reigning monarch, and presents the burning temples and place signs of the cities he conquered (see page 21). But most of the other imperial histories, including

The Aztecs leave the island homeland of Aztlan, and the year count begins, as pictured in the *Codex Mexicanus,* pages 18 and 19 (after the *Journal de la Société des Américanistes* 41 [Paris, 1952]).

The founding of Tenochtitlan, as pictured in the *Codex Mexicanus,* page 44 (after the *Journal de la Société des Américanistes* 41 [Paris, 1952]).

the *Codex Mexicanus,* present a broader range of information. Above the year 4 Reed is the funerary bundle of one ruler and the enthronement of his successor Tizoc, both named glyphically. In the year 6 House, Aztec armies are defeated by the Huexotzinca. When the ruler Tizoc dies in the year 7 Rabbit, his successor Ahuitzotl is seated. The following year the great temple of Tenochtitlan is dedicated. Later the manuscript mentions an earthquake (identified by the convention for movement) in the year 4 Flint. The Aztecs conquered the people of Xochitlan and Amaxtlan in the next two years, where the conquests are designated by the convention for war (the shield and the obsidian-edged club) and the place signs of the two polities. A great flood marks the year 7 Reed; and in 8 Flint, stone was quarried at Malinalco. For most of these events, with the exception of Malinalco and the two conquered cities, the location is not specified. It does not need to be given,

because it is understood, by the people whose history it is, to be Tenochtitlan.

By creating the year-count annal to record their history, the Aztecs located time within the mental conception of Tenochtitlan. History begins when the Aztecs leave Aztlan and continues with the founding of the capital and their imperial rise. The march of the years appears as specifically Aztec time, for the focus is entirely on the Aztecs; named individuals and other polities are included only when their actions affect the Aztecs. In this way, the Aztec annals are narrowly conceived histories of a single people from their own cultural lens.

What the Aztecs have effectively done by using the year-count annal is to make them as a people central to all that occurs. The Aztecs and the city of Tenochtitlan are the unmarked categories; they are considered so fundamental to the history that they need not be named or specifically indicated.

Aztec history from the year 4 Reed to 9 Flint, from the *Codex Mexicanus,* page 71 (after the *Journal de la Société des Américanistes* 41 [Paris, 1952]).

They fill mentally the unpainted surface of all the pages, on which time is essentially an overlay that provides a structure for recording events. The Aztecs used the monotonous sequence of the years to characterize their history and their destiny as an unbroken line. They thus manipulated time both to show the Aztec right to imperial rule and to plant the empire firmly in a deep chronological continuum. The implication carried by the continual march of the years is that the empire is primeval and eternal. By developing the annal format, the Aztecs placed the empire, through its capital at Tenochtitlan, naturally and solidly in a central position with a past, present, and assured future that could be destroyed only by the halting of the years.

The founding of Tenochtitlan itself functioned as a visual and intellectual fulcrum. It occurred in the middle of the Aztec story and was the point where the migration ended and the rise to power

began. Thus it both divided the distant migratory past from the more recent imperial growth and expansion, and became the link between them. Tenochtitlan united deep mythical history with imperial destiny, and in the painted books the founding scene is fundamental to both historical presentations.

More than this, however, the founding event became the icon of the capital city, which itself came to stand for the entire empire. This is seen most clearly in the *Codex Mendoza,* where the year count frames a conceptualized geography that is structurally similar to that of the lienzos (see page 19). The years begin in the upper left corner with the year 2 House and continue down the left side, across the bottom, and then up the right side of the border of blue waters that surround and define the island of Tenochtitlan; running diagonally from corner to corner, the waters of canals cut the city into its four great quarters. At the center of it

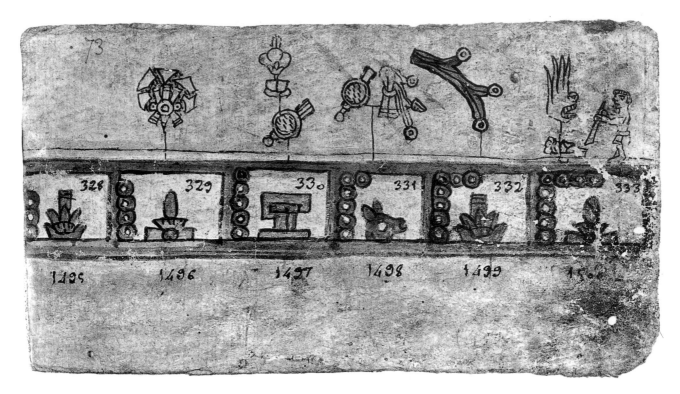

Aztec history from the year 3 Reed to 8 Flint, from the *Codex Mexicanus,* page 73 (after the *Journal de la Société des Américanistes* 41 [Paris, 1952]).

all is the place sign of Tenochtitlan — the nopal cactus growing out of a rock — embellished by the great eagle of the foundation story. Scattered around the place sign and interspersed among the reeds and grasses of the swampy island are the seated figures of the founding clan leaders, all of whom are named with hieroglyphs attached to their shoulders and heads. They give the ancestry of Tenochtitlan. At the bottom of the page, the scenes of two early military victories — over Colhuacan and Tenayuca — point to the victorious future.

In its general aspect, the foundation scene in the *Codex Mendoza* is very much like a lienzo. It establishes the geography and the lineage of the altepetl city of Tenochtitlan, just as the Lienzo de Tequixtepec and the Lienzo de Zacatepec did for those community kingdoms. First it describes the physical setting of the Aztec capital city, picturing the lake, the canals, and the swampy island. Then

it presents and names the city founders and shows the initial conquests that helped to consolidate territory. It serves as a charter for the city, establishing Tenochtitlan geographically and outlining the historical events that were crucial in its early history.

Unlike the lienzos, however, Tenochtitlan in the *Codex Mendoza* has no named boundaries. And this is a key to understanding Moctezuma's view of empire and the place of Tenochtitlan within it. It makes the *Mendoza* presentation more than simply a map of Tenochtitlan at its founding. The painting reveals Moctezuma's view of Tenochtitlan as the center of the known world, and indeed of the cosmos. Because the map gave no boundaries to the city, the waters that surround the island capital metaphorically became the vast waters that surround the earth. The four quarters outlined by the canals then become the four world quarters of the cardinal directions. And they are articulated

172

just as they are in the ritual-divinatory codices, with Tenochtitlan solidly at the center. The altepetl of Tenochtitlan merged conceptually with the territory of the Aztec empire, which also had no borders.

This painting in the *Codex Mendoza* preserves for us the Aztec view that their empire had no geographical limit. It was the center of the spatial world and controlled all the lands around it. Equally, the event and the portrayal of the founding of Tenochtitlan was the historical pivot between the difficult Aztec migration and the glorious imperium that followed. It became the central metaphor for the empire, which the Aztecs saw as enduring as long as time — through the count of the years — continued.

NOTES

1. Bernal Díaz del Castillo, *The Discovery and Conquest of Mexico, 1517–1521,* ed. Genaro García, trans. with notes by A. P. Maudslay, intro. Irving A. Leonard (New York: Farrar, Straus and Cudahy, 1956), p. 72.

2. The passage is paraphrased from J. Eric S. Thompson's translation of Las Casas's torturous Spanish, in *A Commentary on the Dresden Codex* (Philadelphia: Memoirs of the American Philosophical Society, no. 93, 1972), pp. 6–7.

3. *Hernán Cortés: Letters from Mexico,* trans. and ed. Anthony Pagden (New Haven, Conn: Yale University Press, 1986), pp. 340 ff., 354, 367, 386.

4. Johanna Broda has discussed the Aztec idea that hills and mountains contained fertile waters, explaining that the Templo Mayor of Tenochtitlan was conceived as such a sacred mountain. See her "The Provenience of the Sufferings: Tribute and Cosmovisión," in *The Aztec Templo Mayor,* ed. Elizabeth Hill Boone (Washington, D.C.: Dumbarton Oaks, 1987), pp. 211–256.

5. Ross Parmenter, who advised Tequixtepec in this matter, explains the history and discovery of the lienzo and gives a general description of its pictorial features in *Four Lienzos of the Ceixtlahuaca Valley,* Studies in Pre-Columbian Art and Archaeology, no. 26 (Washington, D.C.: Dumbarton Oaks, 1982), pp. 46–62.

6. The lienzo, first published and described in 1900 by Antonio Peñafiel, and has since been insightfully analyzed and explained by Mary Elizabeth Smith in *Picture Writing from Ancient Southern Mexico: Mixtec Place Signs and Maps* (Norman: University of Oklahoma Press, 1973), pp. 89–121.

SELECTED BIBLIOGRAPHY

Armillas, Pedro. "Garden on Swamps." *Science* 174 (1976): 653–661.

———. *Program of the History of American Indians.*Washington, D.C.: Pan American Union, 1958.

Aveni, Anthony F. *Skywatchers of Ancient Mexico.* Austin: University of Texas Press, 1980.

———. *Empires of Time: Calendars, Clocks, and Cultures.* New York: Basic Books, 1989.

Boone, Elizabeth Hill, ed. *The Art and Iconography of Late Post-Classic Central Mexico.* Washington, D.C.: Dumbarton Oaks, 1982.

———, ed. *The Aztec Templo Mayor.* Washington, D.C.: Dumbarton Oaks, 1987.

———, ed. *Ritual Sacrifice in Mesoamerica.* Washington, D.C.: Dumbarton Oaks, 1984.

Broda, Johanna, Davíd Carrasco, and Eduardo Matos Moctezuma. *The Great Temple of Tenochtitlan: Center and Periphery in the Aztec World.* Berkeley: University of California Press, 1987.

Calnek, Edward. "The Internal Structure of Tenochtitlan." In *The Valley of Mexico.* Ed. Eric Wolf. Albuquerque: University of New Mexico Press, 1976.

Carrasco, Davíd. "Aztec Religion." In *The Encyclopedia of Religion.* Ed. Mircea Eliade. Vol. 6, pp. 518–523. New York: Macmillan, 1987.

———. *Quetzalcoatl and the Irony of Empire: Myths and Prophecies in the Aztec Tradition.* Chicago: University of Chicago Press, 1982.

———. *Religions of Mesoamerica: Cosmovision and Ceremonial Centers.* San Francisco: Harper and Row, 1990.

———, ed. *To Change Place: Aztec Ceremonial Landscapes.* Niwot: University Press of Colorado, 1991.

Carrasco, Pedro, and Johanna Broda, eds. *Economía Política e Ideología en el México Prehispánico.* Mexico: Editorial Nueva Imagen, 1978.

Clendinnen, Inga. *Aztecs: An Interpretation.* Cambridge: Cambridge University Press, 1991.

Cortés, Hernán. *Hernán Cortés: Letters from Mexico.* Trans. and ed. Anthony Pagden. New Haven: Yale University Press, 1986.

Davies, Nigel. *The Aztec Empire: The Toltec Resurgence.* Norman: University of Oklahoma Press, 1987.

———. *The Aztecs: A History.* London: Macmillan, 1973.

———. *The Toltec Heritage: From the Fall of Tula to the Rise of Tenochtitlan.* Norman: University of Oklahoma Press, 1980.

———. *The Toltecs: Until the Fall of Tula.* Norman: University of Oklahoma Press, 1977.

Díaz del Castillo, Bernal. *The Discovery and Conquest of Mexico, 1517–1521.* Ed. Genaro García, trans. with notes by A. P. Maudslay, intro. Irving A. Leonard. New York: Farrar, Straus and Cudahy, 1956.

Durán, Fray Diego. *The Aztecs: The History of the Indies of New Spain.* Ed. and trans. Doris Heyden and Fernando Horcasitas. London: Cassell, 1964.

———. *Book of the Gods and Rites and the Ancient Calendar.* Ed. and trans. Fernando Horcasitas and Doris Heyden. Norman: University Press of Oklahoma, 1971.

Eliade, Mircea. *Patterns in Comparative Religion.* New York: World Publishing, 1958.

Gibson, Charles. *The Aztecs Under Spanish Rule: A History of the Indians of the Valley of Mexico, 1519–1810.* Stanford: Stanford University Press, 1964.

Heyden, Doris. "Black Magic: Obsidian in Symbolism and Metaphor." In *Smoke and Mist: Mesoamerican Studies in Memory of Thelma D. Sullivan.* Ed. J. K. Josserand and K. Dakin. Oxford: BAR International Series 402, 1988.

Katz, Friedrich. *Ancient American Civilizations.* New York: Praeger, 1972.

Keen, Benjamin. *The Aztec Image in Western Thought.* New Brunswick, N.J.: Rutgers University Press, 1971.

Klor de Alva, J. Jorge, H. B. Nicholson, and Eloise Quiñones Keber, eds. *The Work of Bernardino de Sahagún, Pioneer Ethnographer of Sixteenth-Century Aztec Mexico.* Albany: Institute for Mesoamerican Studies, State University of New York, 1988.

León-Portilla, Miguel. *Aztec Thought and Culture.* Norman: University of Oklahoma Press, 1963.

———. *The Broken Spears: The Aztec Account of the Conquest of Mexico.* Trans. Lysander Kemp. Boston: Beacon Press, 1962.

———. *Native Mesoamerican Spirituality.* New York: Paulist Press, 1980.

Long, Charles H. *Alpha: The Myths of Creation.* New York: G. Braziller, 1963.

———. *Significations: Signs, Symbols, and Images in the Interpretation of Religion.* Philadelphia: Fortress Press, 1986.

Loo, Peter L. van der. *Códices, Costumbres, Continuidad.* Leiden, 1987.

López Austin, Alfredo. *Hombre-Dios: Religión y Política en el Mundo Nahuatl.* México: Universidad Nacional Autónoma de México, 1973.

———. *The Human Body and Ideology: Concepts of the Ancient Nahuas.* Trans. Thelma Ortiz de Montellano and Bernardo R. Ortiz de Montellano. Salt Lake City: University of Utah Press, 1988.

Matos Moctezuma, Eduardo. *Obras Maestras del Templo Mayor.* México: Fomento Cultural Banamex, 1988.

———. *El Templo Mayor: Excavaciones y Estudios.* México: Instituto Nacional de Antropología e Historia, 1982.

———. *Muerte a Filo de Obsidiana: Los Nahuas Frente a la Muerte.* México: Instituto Nacional de Anthropología e Historia, 1978.

———. *Vida y Muerte en el Templo Mayor.* México: Editorial Océano, 1988.

Nicholson, H. B. "Religion in Pre-Hispanic Central Mexico." In *The Handbook of Middle American Indians,* vol. 10, pp. 395–445. Austin: University of Texas Press, 1964–1976.

———. "Topiltzin Quetzalcoatl of Tollan: A Problem in Meso-american Ethnohistory." Ph.D. diss., Harvard University, 1957.

Ortiz de Montellano, Bernardo R. *Aztec Medicine, Health, and Nutrition.* New Brunswick: Rutgers University Press, 1990.

Pasztory, Esther. *Aztec Art.* New York: Henry N. Abrams, 1983.

Sahagún, Fray Bernardino de. *The Florentine Codex: General History of the Things of New Spain.* Ed. Arthur J.O. Anderson and Charles Dibble. 13 vols. Santa Fe: School of American Research and University of Utah, 1950–1982.

Sanders, William T., Jeffrey R. Parsons, and Robert S. Santley. *The Basin of Mexico: Ecological Processes in the Evolution of a Civilization.* New York: Academic Press, 1979.

Sullivan, Thelma D. "The Rhetorical Orations or Huehuetlatolli, Collected by Sahagún." In *Sixteenth-Century Mexico: The Work of Sahagún.* Ed. Monroe Edmonson. Albuquerque: University of New Mexico Press, 1974.

Townsend, Richard. *State and Cosmos in the Art of Tenochtitlan.* Studies in Pre-Columbian Art and Archaeology, no. 20. Washington, D.C.: Dumbarton Oaks, Trustees for Harvard University, 1979.

GLOSSARY

The Nahuatl Language was phonetically transcribed in the Roman alphabet by Spaniards during the sixteenth century. Nahuatl words usually stress the penultimate syllable.

Vowels are pronounced as in Spanish:

a	as in *far*	*A*catl
e	as in b*e*d	Alt*e*petl
i	as "ee" in d*ee*p	C*i*pactl*i*
o	as in t*o*te	Omete*o*tl
u	as in r*u*le	T*u*la

Consonants are pronounced as in English except:

x	as "sh" in *sh*out	Me*x*ica, *X*ipe Totec
z	as "s" in *s*it	A*z*capotzalco
h	as in *h*it	E*h*ecatl
hu	as "w" in *w*heat	Hue*hu*etl
ll	as in fu*ll*y	O*ll*in
que, qui	as "k" in *k*ite	*Que*tzalcoatl
cu	as "qu" in *qu*it	*Cu*icatl

acatl — "reed," one of twenty day symbols and four year symbols in the Aztec ritual calendar.

Ahuitzotl — eighth Aztec tlatoani who reigned A.D. 1486–1502.

altepetl — "mountain" and "water," Aztec term for "village" or "community."

atl — "water," also one of twenty day symbols in the Aztec ritual calendar.

atl tlachinolli — "water" and "burned," Aztec metaphor meaning; "warfare."

Axayacatl — sixth Aztec tlatoani, who reigned A.D. 1469–1481.

Azcapotzalco — powerful Tepanec city that dominated the lake region when the Mexica first arrived in the area. The Aztecs were vassals of and paid tribute to Azcapotzalco up until they conquered the city.

Aztlan — mythical homeland of the Aztecs to the north, where the Mexica ancestors began their migration.

calli — "house," one of twenty day symbols and four year symbols in the Aztec ritual calendar.

calmecac — temple schools for the Aztec nobility.

calpixque — tribute collectors of the Aztec empire.

calpuleque — the chiefs of calpullis, or one of the clans that made up Tenochtitlan.

calpulli, calpultin — one of the kin-based social groups or clans that were subdivisions making up the city of Tenochtitlan. They had their own temples and schools; they organized community labor; and they provided warriors in times of war.

Cemanahuac — "Land Surrounded by Water," Aztec term for the terrestrial level of the cosmos.

centzon huitznahua — the "four hundred Southerners," siblings of Coyolxauhqui in the myth of Coatepec, and metaphor representing the stars in the night sky.

chacmool — term used for the Toltec-style reclining seated sculptures found at the Great Temple of Tenochtitlan (Mayan term).

Chapultepec — "Grasshopper Hill," where the

Mexica settled on the western shore of Lake Texcoco before founding Tenochtitlan.

Chicomoztoc — "Place of the Seven Caves," mythic place of origin of the Aztecs and their deities.

chinampa — agricultural system of intensive cultivation that supported urban centers in the lake region.

Cihuacoatl — "Women Serpent," Aztec earth and mother goddess.

cihuateteo — "women who died during childbirth."

cihuatlampa — "region of women," the west.

cipactli — "alligator," the earth monster on whose back the world rested, also the first day symbol in the Aztec ritual calendar.

Cipactonal — one of the creator deities who, along with Omoxoco, created the first human couple, provided them with weaving and agriculture, determined the structure of the universe, and created the calendar.

citlalco — "region where the stars are found," the second celestial level in Aztec cosmology.

citlalcuitlatl — "star excrement," meteorites.

citlalin popoca — "smoking stars," comets or meteors.

citlalocuile — "star caterpillars."

citlaltlachtli — "celestial ball court," possibly the constellation, Gemini.

coa — traditional digging stick used in Mesoamerican agriculture (Arawak term).

Coatepec, Coatepetl — "Serpent Mountain," mythical birthplace of Huitzilopochtli and name given by the Aztecs to their greatest shrine, the Great Temple of Tenochtitlan.

coatl — "serpent," one of the twenty day signs in the Aztec ritual calendar.

Coatlicue — "Woman with the Serpent Skirt," mother of Huitzilopochtli in the Myth of Coatepec, Aztec earth goddess of life and of death.

colotl ixayac — possibly the constellation Scorpio.

Coyolxauhqui — "Woman with Copper Bells," warrior daughter of Coatlicue slain and dismembered by her brother Huitzilopochtli in the myth of Coatepec. She also represents the moon in Aztec mythology.

Cuauhtemoc — the last Aztec tlatoani, who tried unsuccessfully to defend the city of Tlatelolco against Spanish attack in 1521.

cuauhxicalli — "eagle vessel," Aztec stone sculptures in a variety of forms used to contain sacrificed human hearts.

cuicacalli — "house of songs," institution established to provide music, dance, and theater for the Aztec festivals.

cuicatl — "songs," in this case, "birdsongs."

Ehecatl — Aztec Lord of the Wind, an apparition of Quetzalcoatl, the Feathered Serpent.

Huehueteotl — the "Old God," Aztec Lord of Fire.

huehuetl — Aztec sacred vertical wooden drum.

huehuetlatolli — the "ancient words" or "sayings of the elders," elegant rhetorical orations representing the traditional teachings about ethics, aesthetics, symbolism, politics, and authority in the Aztec world.

Huitzilopochtli — "Hummingbird on the Left" or "to the South," patron deity of the Mexica and Aztec god of the sun and of war.

Huitznahua — the clan led by Coyolxauhqui in the myth of Coatepec.

Huixtocihuatl — Aztec deity of salt.

Itzapapalotl — "Obsidian Butterfly," earth goddess of war and sacrifice by obsidian knife.

Itzcoatl — fourth Aztec tlatoani who reigned A.D. 1427–1440.

macehual, macehualtin — the Aztec class of commoners.

Malinalco — site of an important Aztec religious shrine that according to Aztec myth was founded by Malinalxochitl, the sorceress sister of Huitzilopochtli.

mayeque — a social group of agricultural workers who worked another's land and paid taxes to the owner.

Mexica — the ethnic group who, after a great migration from the north, settled in the lake region, first at Chapultepec, then at Tenochtitlan, Tlatelolco, and Malinalco, and later dominated the Aztec empire.

Mictecacihuatl — "Lady of the Underworld," the Aztec goddess of death.

mictlampa — "region of the dead," the underworld.

Mictlan — the ninth level of the underworld, where the souls of people who died ordinary deaths resided.

Mictlantecuhtli — "Lord of the Underworld," Aztec god of death.

milli — plowed or worked fields.

Moctezuma Ilhuicamina (Moctezuma I) — fifth Aztec tlatoani, who reigned A.D. 1440–1464.

Moctezuma Xocoyotzin (Moctezuma II) — ninth Aztec tlatoani, who reigned A.D. 1502–1520.

Nezahualcoyotl — the "Fasting Coyote," poet- philosopher-ruler of the cultural center, Texcoco.

Nezahualpilli — the "Fasting Prince," astrologer-ruler of Texcoco who interpreted the bad omen that the comet represented to Moctezuma II.

Omecihuatl, Ometeotl — "Masters of Duality," Aztec goddess and god who created Quetzalcoatl and the three Tezcatlipocas.

Omeyocan — "Place of Duality," the twelfth and thirteenth celestial levels in Aztec cosmology.

Oxomoco — one of the creator deities who, along with Cipactonal, created the first human couple, provided them with weaving and agriculture, determined the structure of the universe, and created the ritual calendar.

oyohualli — small bells worn by the four hundred Southerners in the myth of Coatepec.

pilli, pipiltin — Aztec nobles, or the nobility.

pochteca — tradesmen or merchant-warriors who penetrated unconquered lands and served as spies for the Aztec empire.

Quetzalcoatl — "Feathered Serpent," important Aztec deity with complex symbolism.

tecpatl — sacrificial flint knife.

temalacatl — "circular stone" used for gladiatorial sacrifices.

Tenochtitlan — imperial capital of the Aztec empire founded by the Mexica around A.D. 1325.

teocalli — an Aztec temple.

Teotihuacan — "Abode (or Birthplace) of the Gods," important archaeological site in central Mexico known to the Aztecs.

Tepanec — a powerful alliance of communities that dominated the lake region when the Mexica first settled in the Valley of Mexico (Nahuatl: Tepaneca).

tepetl — "mountain."

tepochcalli — school where the Aztec nobility learned arts and crafts to augment their military and religious training.

teponaxtli — Aztec horizontal drum.

tetecuhtin — members of the nobility who achieved their status by excelling in war.

teyolia — Aztec term for the spiritual force that resided in the human heart and provided the person with intelligence, fondness, and inclinations.

Tezcatlipoca — "Smoking Mirror," an important Aztec deity related to warfare, rulership, magic, and the night.

Tianquiztli — "Marketplace," the star cluster known to us as Pleiades.

Tizoc — seventh Aztec tlatoani who reigned A.D. 1481–1486.

tlacuillos — artists who painted the Mesoamerican screenfold manuscripts.

Tlahuizcalpantecuhtli — an Aztec deity representing the planet Venus and a apparition of Quetzacoatl, the Feathered Serpent.

Tlaloc — important Aztec rain and fertility deity, to whom the north side of the Great Temple at Tenochtitlan was dedicated.

Tlalocan — Tlaloc's paradise, where individuals who died from water-related causes would reside after death.

Tlaloque — the servants of Tlaloc.

Tlaltecuhtli — the Aztec lord of the earth, or earth monster.

tlamatinime — "knowers of things," Aztec wise men who used language arts to seek and teach profound truths.

Tlatelolco — Mexica city just north of Tenochtitlan,

where the great marketplace of the Aztec empire was located.

tlatoani — "first speaker," king or emperor of the Aztec empire who was elected by the Aztec nobility.

Tlaxcala — polity that resisted conquest by the Aztecs and allied with the Spaniards to conquer Tenochtitlan and Tlatelolco (Spanish spelling of Tlaxcallan).

tochtli — "rabbit," also one of the twenty day symbols and four year symbols of the Aztec ritual calendar.

Tollan — "Place of Reeds," capital of the previous Toltec empire in Aztec myths.

Tonacacihuatl — "Lady of Sustenance," Aztec creator deity.

Tonacatecuhtli — "Lord of Sustenance," Aztec creator deity.

Tonalamatl — "book of days," depiction of the ritual calendar in Mesoamerican pictorial manuscripts.

Tonatiuh — Aztec solar deity, the "Fifth Sun."

Topiltzin Quetzalcoatl — "Our Young Prince the Feathered Serpent," the priest-ruler of Tollan in Aztec myths, who was banished from that city but vowed to return.

Toxiuhmolpilia — the "Binding of the Years," the Aztec New Fire Ceremony.

tzompantli — Aztec "skull rack" found at the Great Temple of Tenochtitlan.

Xilonen — the young Aztec maize goddess.

Xipe Totec — "Our Lord the Flayed One," Aztec god of spring and of rebirth.

Xiuhcoatl — "fire serpent."

Xiuhtecuhtli — Aztec fire deity, lord of the hearth.

xihuitl — meaning "year," "turquoise," "grass," or "comet," and a metaphor for "precious time."

Xochimilco — community located on the lakeshore to the south of Tenochtitlan, where chinampa agricultural production took place.

xochitl — "flower," also one of twenty day signs in the Aztec ritual calendar.

yohualitqui mamalhuaztli — "fire-drilling stick."

zacatapayolli — the "grass ball of human sacrifice."

CONTRIBUTORS

DAVÍD CARRASCO is a historian of religions, director of the Mesoamerican Archive, University of Colorado, Boulder, and author of *Quetzalcoatl and the Irony of Empire: Myths and Prophecies in the Aztec Tradition* plus *Religions of Mesoamerica: Cosmovision and Ceremonial Centers,* and editor and contributor for *To Change Place: Aztec Ceremonial Landscapes.*

EDUARDO MATOS MOCTEZUMA is professor of archaeology at the Instituto Nacional de Antropología e Historia and director of the Museo del Templo Mayor in Mexico City. He was general coordinator of Proyecto Templo Mayor and Proyecto Tlatelolco. He is the author of many works, including *Vida y Muerte en el Templo Mayor* and *Muerte a Filo de Obsidiana: Los Nahuas Frente a la Muerte.*

ANTHONY F. AVENI, Russell B. Colgate Professor of astronomy and anthropology at Colgate University, is one of the pioneers of archaeoastronomical studies. He has published numerous works, including *Skywatchers of Ancient Mexico* and *Empires of Time.*

ELIZABETH HILL BOONE is director of Pre-Columbian Studies at Dumbarton Oaks, Washington, D.C., editor of *The Aztec Templo Mayor,* and author of *The Codex Magliabechiano and the Lost Prototype of the Magliabechiano Group.*

JAMES N. CORBRIDGE, JR., is Chancellor of the University of Colorado, Boulder. He received his BA degree from Brown University in 1955 and his LL.B. from Yale Law School in 1963. Corbridge has been a Visiting Scholar at the Institute for Advanced Legal Studies at the University of London, and a Visiting Scholar at the University of Linköping, Sweden.

SALVADOR GUIL'LIEM ARROYO is an archaeologist and photographer active in the excavations at the Templo Mayor and Tlatelolco in Mexico City. He is chief photographer for *Moctezuma's Mexico.*

SCOTT SESSIONS is a senior research assistant at the Mesoamerican Archive, University of Colorado, Boulder. He is a graduate student in the Department of History and is studying narrative strategies in pre-hispanic and colonial manuscripts of Mexico.

INDEX